INDEX

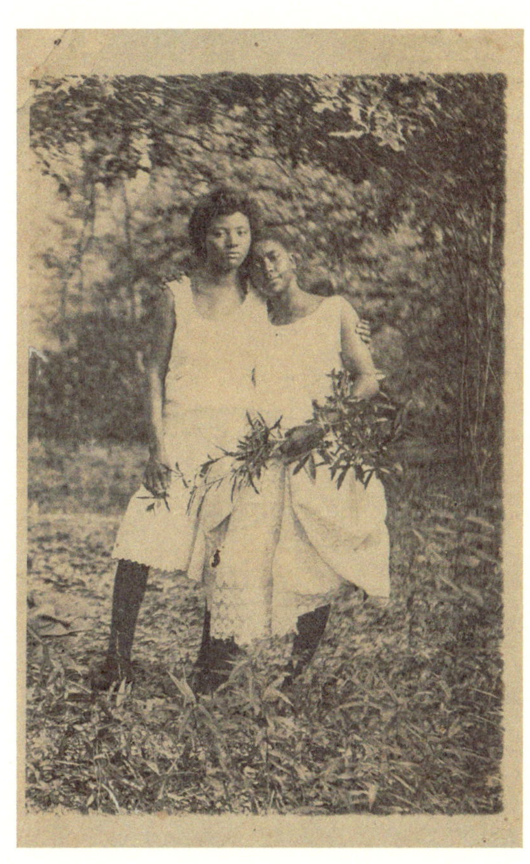

Love, You Came From Greatness

ARTIST NYDIA BLAS, CURATOR KATE ADDLEMAN-FRANKEL,
AND SCHOLAR AND WRITER CHERYL FINLEY IN CONVERSATION

This book emerged from a commission by the Johnson Museum of Art, Cornell University, for the artist to create and exhibit a new body of work in dialogue with historical African-American family albums held by the Cornell Library.

CF   One of the things that I love about your portraiture, Nydia, is the way in which family has inspired the work that you do. Family as a point of inspiration, a point of pride, a point of solace, a point of meditation on the archive of family, and the family as archive. The way you know who the individuals in these photographs are, know what the occasions are, makes me think about how, in vernacular photography, or portrait photography, particularly in Black communities, there are certain ways in which we honor one another, honor the people that we love and care about. Love is the first word in the title, and love is so much about who you, Nydia, are as an individual.

      When I saw some of the historic family photographs that peppered your house, that you were surrounded by, I saw that there are ones that honor not just individual family members, but also the kinds of things that we take pride in. Like owning a home in downtown Ithaca, or owning a car, or celebrating a particular occasion that is one to be proud of. I see you honoring your aunt, Beverly J. Martin, who has an elementary school named after her, and who went to Cornell, and was an activist. Those are the kinds of things that are secreted within you as someone who grew up in and around Ithaca, so heavily influenced by many of these people.

NB   I'm sitting here, nodding my head at the words "pride" and "proud."
My first reaction when I looked at the book was an overwhelming sense of
pride. It made me cry. But it's complicated. It hits on all these different notes.
When I think of a portrait, I'm immediately thinking of our history, and the
gaze. Especially the gazes of Black girls and women, creating a powerful space
from which to look back. It feels strong. It feels confident. And then, some of
it is negating the gaze completely. What does it mean when the subjects' eyes
are covered, or they're not able to look back? I've always been really interested
in this space that says "There is no agency."

          Or is there? Negating the gaze can create another space of *interior*
experience, where the subject is dealing with herself. Where she's not even
concerned about the person that's looking on. Not, "You get to look at me and
objectify me," but, "I'm not even considering you."

CF   I wonder how you were exposed to photography. Whether it was in
the home or in the 7th grade, or in photographing your children as a young
mother, and then later studying photography at Ithaca College and then
Syracuse University.

NB   I've always just loved family photographs. They meant so much to
me and shaped my entire life. It's probably why I'm a photographer. Period.
Because I was surrounded by portraits and they really did serve as a proof.
We all know that a photograph is tied to the truth in some way—that pride of
owning a house or owning a car. But also, I'm always thinking about, "Who's
the photographer?" because there are some really good compositions in some
of my family albums, and a certain aesthetic that comes up in my own work too.

KA-F   One of the most striking things about your images is that they don't
only make a clear and explicit connection to everyday family photographs, the
kind we all have and look at. They also make manifest the exceptional side of
those images—the wondrousness and the mystery contained particularly in
photographs we didn't take or weren't around for, that in part makes them
so powerful. Your work for this project really captured the experience of the
family photograph as an enigma.

NB   I think I made the connection to my family albums when I was studying at Syracuse and working on *The Girls Who Spun Gold* consistently for
three years. I put all those photographs up and thought, "What did I just do?"

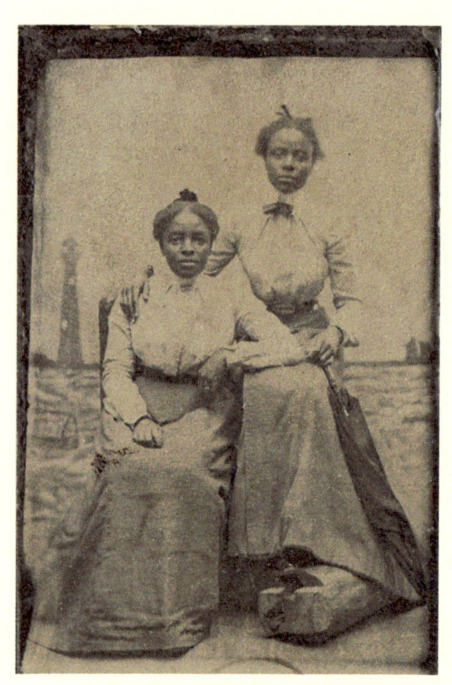

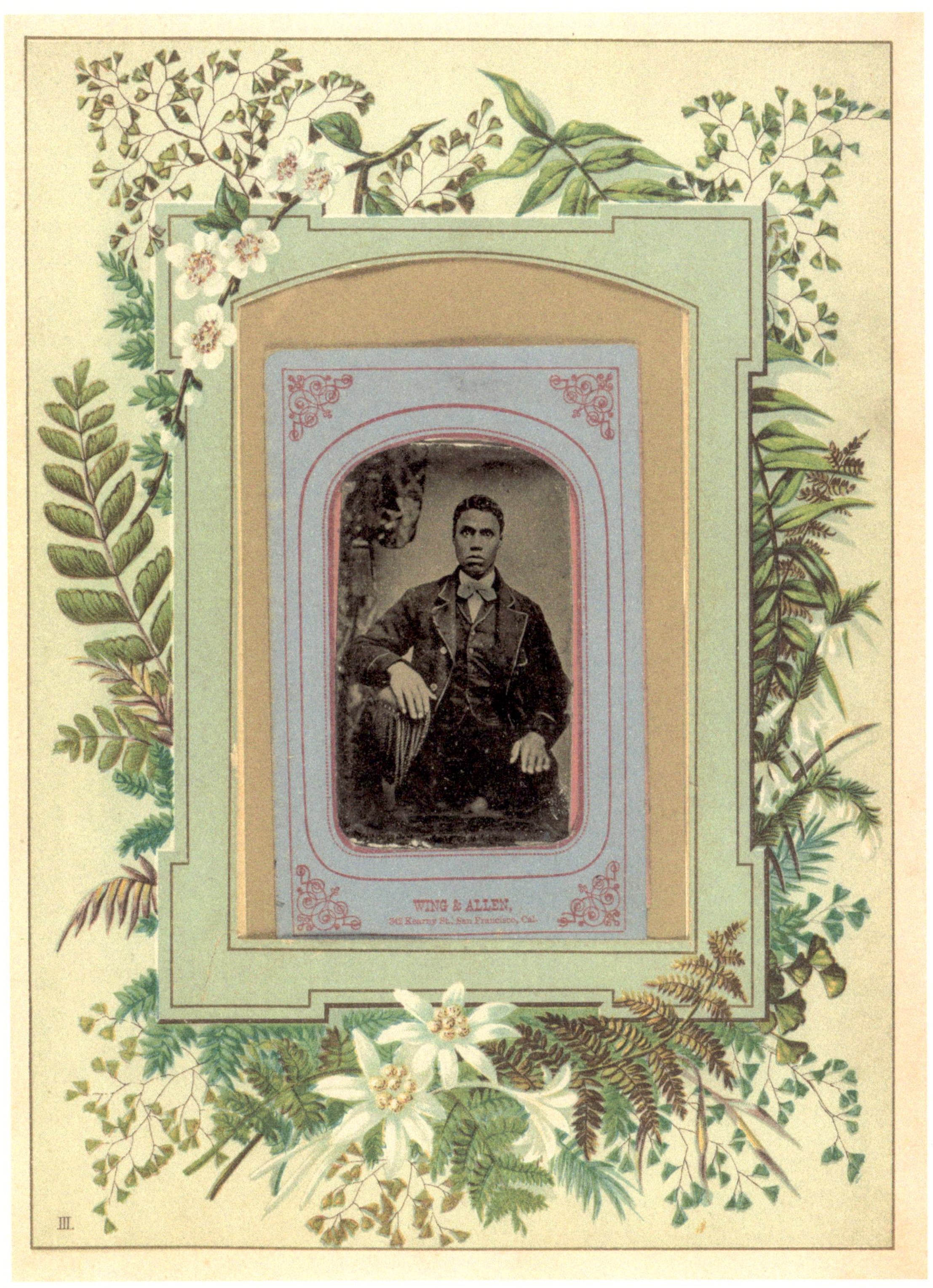

WING & ALLEN,
343 Kearny St., San Francisco, Cal.
III.

And how do I talk about this? I asked myself, what was the first image I'd ever seen? What was the first photograph I'd ever seen? And that's when I started understanding those family photos and the important role they played.

I was always photographing people that I knew, and it was always portraits, from the very beginning. A portrait is a mediation between myself and the subject. There's something that I see in them that I want to pull out. But then there's also who they are. So you find these in-between moments.

KA-F   I think it's important to describe your approach to this project. We commissioned you to make new work in response to the family albums in Cornell's library, but were not prescriptive about what kind of work it would be. The idea to photograph families in Ithaca came from you. I love how you formulated the idea that you were contributing to a theoretical album of Black family life in the United States, an album that would be very broad and messy and multifaceted, and that would contain you and your perspective, and in which Ithaca and this community would be represented through your work.

CF   As to the archival materials that were included in the exhibition, well, it takes a while for people to really understand that work in the present. How to make sense of it. How to use it as a way to understand one's community.

KA-F   Yes. Thanks, Cheryl. There are a lot of attendant questions around the collection of those kinds of materials—materials that belonged to Black families or to other oppressed communities—by institutions, particularly white institutions or institutions that historically marginalized those communities, as opposed to Black institutions like Spelman [where Finley and Blas are both professors]. I think we have a responsibility to the artifacts and an ethical imperative to do what we can to reconnect them to the communities they've been separated from, to activate them in a responsible way. Having an artist engage with these albums, specifically Nydia, a Black woman from Ithaca, turned them into something that could be tangibly connected with the Black community here.

We had never done anything like this at the Johnson before, and I think it could provide a model for us to follow. We were really excited about the results—the work itself of course, and also the community's response to it when we exhibited it at the museum. Nydia's artist's talk for the show was a major event!

CF   It reminds me a little bit of the invitation that was made to Fred
Wilson in the early '90s to go to the Maryland Historical Society to look into
their archives and create an exhibition. He ended up creating the exhibition
"Mining the Museum" that really changed the way the Historical Society
thought about its collections. Wilson highlighted everything from a silver tea
service to a set of shackles, to a KKK hood and a baby carriage, to finely crafted
furniture to a whipping post. It not only transformed the Historical Society in
Maryland, but changed the way that he as an artist worked, and changed the
way that many other institutions that have historical collections worked. It
created a conversation that really lends importance both to the lives that we
live in the present and to how we understand ourselves with respect to what's
held in archives. Other examples include Kara Walker, who, I know, is an artist that has been very influential for you, Nydia. In 2006, at the Metropolitan
Museum of Art, she had an exhibition called "After the Deluge," where she
went into their collection and curated an exhibition that also included, and
reimagined, some of her own work.

        I am also thinking about the question of the history of photography
and especially portraiture and I'm thinking about people like Deborah Willis,
who is both an artist herself and an acclaimed historian of photography, particularly African American photography. Willis cut her teeth at the Schomburg
Center for Research in Black Culture, which brings me back to your point,
Katie, around the responsibility of art institutions. What's the ethical call for
Predominantly White Institutions to collect material that pertains to under-
represented people, whether it's demographically in a region or within their
own collections? How do we deal with those kinds of collections? But, back to
Willis for a minute, her hive of scholarship around portraiture as practice and
how photographic portraits of Black people have been a practice since the
very beginning of the history of photography to the present is a framework
within which Nydia's work most definitely falls.

KA-F   I'm glad you brought up Deb Willis. She is an exceptional scholar
and we owe so much to her.

CF   I'm also thinking about the work of James Van Der Zee. If we're
going to talk about portrait photography, he's an obvious person to bring into
Nydia's conversation around spirituality and magic. Especially some of those
images from *The Harlem Book of the Dead* or even the wedding portraits.
Yes, they are constructed. They are studio portraits. But he goes above and

beyond—retouching the negatives, adding heavenly bodies, things to embellish the images, their lives, their legacies. Many of the goals of Van Der Zee as an artist, photographer, or documentarian worked to push back against this other, shadow archive of negativity, which is why it was so important for him to sometimes outfit or costume the people that he photographed.

NB   I've always thought of my own work as creating a sort of counter-narrative. And I've thought of James Van Der Zee in relation to my constructed work, like *The Girls Who Spun Gold*. Controlling all the elements, the location, the clothing as costume. It's a marker. It stands in for other things, like status. And then the gesture or the action. And how all those things come together to make a really powerful portrait.

I've always felt: give me a camera and I'm gonna try to make it interesting. In my own practice, I've leaned towards the image that is constructed. My roots are probably more in the documentary tradition, but it got to a point where I wanted to be able to construct my own image. I wanted to make photographs of Black people and I wanted them to say something specific as it relates to race, gender, sexuality. And so how can I do those things? I can make pictures of Black people.

Then I started doing editorial work, which was mostly portraits of Black women that make them look strong, because that was what I liked to do and have been asked to do. Those images sit in this interesting space of construction and documentation. For this project with the Johnson Museum and the body of work in the book, I started with a list of places that I was interested in, like a porch, a living room—thinking about how those spaces are invitational spaces, intimate spaces, that cross public and private. I was really looking at those spaces as themes. I was looking for a space between something super constructed and the documentary. At first I liked the ones that felt more magical, like the image on the cover. But then finding that space where my pictures were more in conversation with the original historical albums, was interesting. So I can set the initial scene or idea, but then let something more natural happen in that space.

In this project, I notice that I really love photographing green and lush spaces with water and trees. It can look magical, but it left me with this sense that Ithaca likes to think that it is this magical space where people buy local and all the wonderful things, and that it is exempt from the problems of the world. But this is a negation of real problems. When I come back to Ithaca, I'm like, What?! All of these difficult issues are very much also a part of Ithaca.

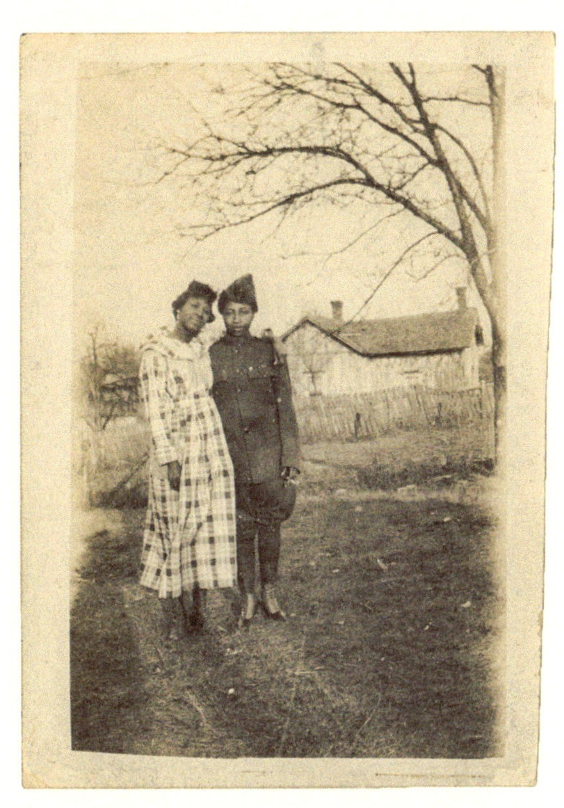

I just keep thinking Ithaca, Ithaca, Ithaca, Ithaca is the one through line. We started with the new images I had made in Ithaca and then the old images of my family that's lived there for 100 years. When I left Ithaca, I was really mad at Ithaca. And when I did this project, I was like, oh, no, how am I going to talk shit about Ithaca in my work, in a way that's beneficial? How am I really going to talk about this? How am I gonna say the truths about Ithaca and the damage that it caused me? And say it in my own terms. Because when I left, I was like, man, forget this place. I'm in Atlanta now and it feels so different. There was this level of angst that left my body. Leaving a predominantly white space and coming to Atlanta, I woke up every day and was happy. It was just a completely different energy. So when I was going back to make this work, every single time, I healed something in me. I love thinking about the notion of making something to heal something in you.

CF   You told me, As long as you have been an artist, you've been a mom. Maybe there's something that you might say about that experience and how it remains a part of your practice?

NB   Yeah, I had a non-traditional route to my education and career. I got married and had my son at 18. And then, five years later, had my daughter Rosario. And then I decided: I'm going to school, as I don't like working for other people. I went to TC3 [Tompkins County Community College, in Ithaca], but then I thought, I can't study photography because that's really irresponsible. I have kids now, right? And then I got a camera and went on a trip to Guatemala for two weeks and after that I was like, OK, I'm supposed to… I HAVE to do this. This is what I'm supposed to do. I came back and enrolled in photo classes and really committed to what I needed to do. I met Ahndraya Parlato because she was my professor at TC3, and even in my first photography class, with her, I was photographing my nieces. And with my first camera, I was always photographing my family, the people that I knew, the people that were around me. Sometimes it feels more like a collaboration with somebody you know. Sometimes I'm asking my subject to, say, take off their shirt and twist their sister's arms. So there has to be some comfort and some type of exchange. And I feel thankful that my life went the way that it did, because when I was making images I felt like I had life to comment on. I had feelings and experiences and these children and I'm a single mom and this is complicated and they're there. So, as a parent, I'm thinking: do my homework, cook dinner, photograph my kids. As if my life had always been like that.

As if I asked myself, with this cramped schedule, how do I maintain relationships and also use photography as a connecting tool?

One way I am thinking about authority is through storytelling, through the ability to tell a story in order to take charge of something. In one of my first weeks teaching at Spelman I was sitting in the back of the room while showing a film, and I was crying because I had never been in a room full of Black women learning about photography—*a room full*—in my entire education. Never. Unless it was a space that I created for myself, or for other people. The first thing that I always have my students read in class is bell hooks' essay "The Oppositional Gaze: Black Female Spectators" (1992). It is so important to keep saying that there is power in looking, and that your viewpoint is really important. And that what you have to say is really important. For Black women, we've learned not to take charge or not to think that the things that we are making, or the things that we have to say, are important. So, there's this really special authority that happens when you have a camera because you're in charge, you're the boss, you're the one in control.

Nydia Blas. Photographer. MFA (Syracuse), Assistant Professor in the Department of Art and Visual Culture at Spelman College.

Kate Addleman-Frankel. PhD. (University of Toronto). Gary and Ellen Davis Curator of Photography at the Herbert F. Johnson Museum of Art, Cornell University.

Cheryl Finley. Scholar and Writer. Ph.D (Yale), Inaugural Director of the Atlanta University Center Art History + Curatorial Studies Collective; Distinguished Visiting Professor in the Department of Art & Visual Culture at Spelman College, and Associate Professor in the Department of History of Art and Visual Studies at Cornell University.

Historical Images courtesy the Stephan Loewentheil Photograph Collection, #8043. Division of Rare and Manuscript Collections, Cornell University Library

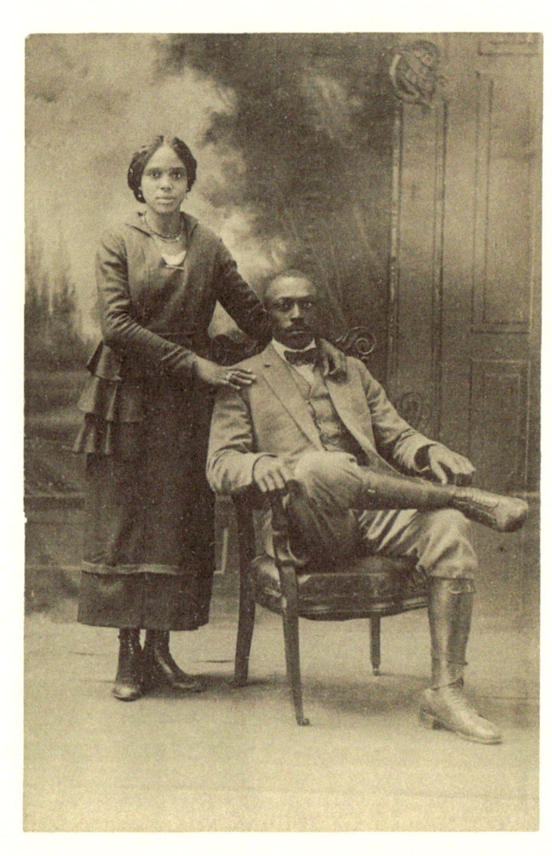

In Our Glory:
Photography and Black Life

bell hooks

Always a daddy's girl. I was not surprised that my sister V. became a lesbian, or that her lovers were always white women. Her worship of Daddy and her passion for whiteness appeared to affirm a movement away from black womanhood and, of course, away from that image of the woman we did not want to become—our mother. The only family photograph V. displays in her house is a picture of our dad, looking young with a mustache. His dark skin mingling with the shadows in the photograph. All of which is highlighted by the white T-shirt he wears.

In this snapshot he is standing by a pool table. The look on his face is confident, seductive, cool—a look we rarely saw growing up. I have no idea who took the picture, only that it pleases me to imagine that he cared for the person—deeply. There is such boldness, such fierce openness in the way he faces the camera. This snapshot was taken before marriage, before us, his seven children, before our presence in his life forced him to leave behind the carefree masculine identity this pose conveys.

The fact that my sister V. possesses this image of our dad, one that I had never seen before, merely affirms their romance, the bond between the two of them. They had the dreamed-about closeness between father and daughter, or so it seemed. Her possession of the snapshot confirms this, is an acknowledgment that she is allowed to know—yes, even to possess—that private life he always kept to himself. When we were children, he refused to answer our questions about who he was, how he acted, what he did and felt before us. It was as though he did not want to remember or share that part of himself, as though remembering hurt. Standing before this snapshot, I come closer to the cold, distant, dark man who is my father, closer than I can ever come in real life. Not always able to love him there, I am sure I can love this version of him the snapshot. I gave it a title: "in his glory."

Before leaving my sister's place, I plead with her to make a copy of this picture for my birthday. She says she will, but it never comes. For Christmas, then. It's on the way. I surmise that my passion for it surprises her, makes her hesitate. My rival in childhood—she always winning, the possessor of Dad's affection—she wonders whether to give that up, whether she is ready to share. She hesitates to give me the man in the snapshot. After all, had he wanted me to see him this way, "in his glory," he would have given me the picture.

My younger sister G. calls. For Christmas, V. has sent her a "horrible photograph" of Dad. There is outrage in her voice as she says, "It's disgusting. He's not even wearing a shirt, just an old white undershirt."

G. keeps repeating, "I don't know why she has sent this picture to me." She has no difficulty promising to give me her copy if mine does not arrive. Her lack of interest in the photograph saddens me. When she was the age our dad is in the picture, she looked just like him. She had his beauty then, the same shine of glory and pride. Is this the face of herself that she has forgotten, does not want to be reminded of, because time has taken such glory away? Unable to fathom how she cannot be drawn to this picture, I ponder what this image suggests to her that she cannot tolerate: a grown black man having a good time, playing a game, having a drink maybe, enjoying himself without the company of women.

Although my sisters and I look at this snapshot and see the same man, we do not see him in the same way. Our "reading" and experience of this image is shaped by our relationship with him, with the world of childhood and the images that make our lives what they are now. I want to rescue and preserve this image of our father, not let it be forgotten. It allows me to understand him, provides a way for me to know him that makes it possible to love him again, despite all the other images, the ones that stand in the way of love.

Such is the power of the photograph, of the image, that it can give back and take away, that it can bind. This snapshot of Veodis Watkins, our father, sometimes called Ned or Leakey in his younger days, gives me a space for intimacy between the image and myself, between me and Dad. I am captivated, seduced by it, the way other images have caught and held me, embraced me like arms that would not let go.

Struggling in childhood with the image of myself as unworthy of love, I could not see myself beyond all the received images, which simply reinforced my sense of unworthiness. Those ways of seeing myself came from voices of authority. The place where I could see myself, beyond imposed images, was in the realm of the snapshot. I am most real to myself in snapshots—there I see an image I can love.

My favorite childhood snapshot, then and now, showed me in costume, masquerading. Long after it had disappeared, I continued to long for it, and to grieve. I loved this snapshot of myself because it was the only image available to me that gave me a sense of presence, of girlhood beauty and capacity for pleasure. It was an image of myself I could genuinely like. At that stage of my life I was crazy about Westerns, about cowboys and Indians. The camera captured me in my cowgirl outfit, white ruffled blouse, vest, fringed skirt, my one gun and my boots. In this image I became all that I wanted to be in my imagination.

For a moment, suspended in this image: I am a cowgirl. There is a look of heavenly joy on my face. I grew up needing this image, cherishing it—my one reminder that there was a precious little girl inside me able to know and express joy. I took this photograph with me on a visit to the house of my father's cousin Schuyler.

His was a home where art and the image mattered. No wonder, then, that I wanted to share my "best" image. Making my first real journey away from home, from a small town to my first big city, I needed the security of this image. I packed it carefully. I wanted Lovie, cousin Schuyler's wife, to see me "in my glory." I remember giving her the snapshot for safekeeping: only, when it was time for me to return home, it could not be found. This was for me a terrible loss, an irreconcilable grief. Gone was the image of myself I could love. Losing that snapshot, I lost the proof of my worthiness—that I had ever been a bright-eyed child capable of wonder— the proof that there was a "me of me."

The image in this snapshot has lingered in my mind's eye for years. It has lingered there to remind me of the power of snapshots, of the image. As I slowly complete a book of essays titled *Art on My Mind*, I think about the place of art in black life, connections between the social construction of black identity, the impact of race and class, and the presence in black life of an inarticulate but ever-present visual aesthetic governing our relationship to images, to the process of image making. I return to the snapshot as a starting point to consider the place of the visual in black life—the importance of photography.

Cameras gave to black folks, irrespective of class, a means by which we could participate fully in the production of images. Hence it is essential that any theoretical discussion of the relationship of black life to the visual, to art making, make photography

central. Access and mass appeal have historically made photography a powerful location for the construction of an oppositional black aesthetic. Before racial integration there was a constant struggle on the part of black folks co create a counterhegemonic world of images that would stand as visual resistance, challenging racist images. All colonized and subjugated people who, by way of resistance, create an oppositional subculture within the framework of domination recognize that the field of representation (how we see ourselves, how others see us) is a site of ongoing struggle.

The history of black liberation movements in the United States could be characterized as a struggle over images as much as it has also been a struggle for rights, for equal access. To many reformist black civil rights activists, who believed that desegregation would offer the humanizing context that would challenge and change white supremacy, the issue of representation—control over images—was never as important as equal access. As time has progressed and the face of white supremacy has not changed, reformist and radical blacks would likely agree that the field of representation remains a crucial realm of struggle, as important as the question of equal access, if not more important. Roger Wilkins emphasizes this point in his recent essay "White Out."

Though our politics differ, Wilkins's observations echo my insistence, in the opening essay of *Black Looks: Race and Representation*, that black people have made few, if any, revolutionary interventions in the arena of representation. In part, racial desegregation—equal access—offered a vision of racial progress that, however limited, led many black people to be less vigilant about the question of representation. Concurrently, contemporary commodification of blackness creates a market context wherein conventional, even stereotypical, modes of representing blackness may receive the greatest reward. This leads to a cultural context in which images that would subvert the status quo are harder to produce. There is no "perceived market" for them. Nor should it surprise us that the erosion of oppositional black subcultures (many of which have been destroyed in the desegregation process) has deprived us of those sites of radical resistance where we have had primary control over representation. Significantly, nationalist black freedom movements were often concerned only with questions of "good" and "bad" imagery and did not promote a more expansive cultural understanding of the politics of representation. Instead they promoted notions of essence and identity that ultimately restricted and confined black image production.

No wonder, then, that racial integration has created a crisis in black life, signaled by the utter loss of critical vigilance in the arena of image making—by our being stuck in endless debate over good and bad imagery. The aftermath of this crisis has been devastating in that it has led to a relinquishment of collective black interest in the production of images. Photography began to have less significance in black life as a means—private or public—by which an oppositional standpoint could be asserted, a mode of seeing different from that of the dominant culture. Everyday black folks began to see themselves as not having a major role to play in the production of images.

To reverse this trend we must begin to talk about the significance of black image production in daily life prior to racial integration. When we concentrate on photography, then, we make it possible to see the walls of photographs in black homes as a critical intervention, a disruption of white control over black images.

Most Southern black folks grew up in a context where snapshots and the more stylized photographs taken by professional photographers were the

easiest images to produce. Displaying these images in everyday life was as central as making them. The walls of images in Southern black homes were sites of resistance. They constituted private, black-owned and -operated gallery space where images could be displayed, shown to friends and strangers. These walls were a space where, in the midst of segregation, the hardship of apartheid, dehumanization could be countered. Images could be critically considered, subjects positioned according to individual desire.

Growing up inside these walls, many of us did not, at the time, regard them as important or valuable. Increasingly, as black folks live in a world so technologically advanced that it is possible for images to be produced and reproduced instantly, it is even harder for some of us to emotionally contextualize the significance of the camera in black life during the years of racial apartheid. The sites of contestation were not out there, in the world of white power, they were within segregated black life. Since no "white" galleries displayed images of black people created by black folks, spaces had to be made within diverse black communities. Across class boundaries black folks struggled with the issue of representation. This issue was linked with the issue of documentation; hence the importance of photography. The camera was the central instrument by which blacks could disprove representations of us created by white folks. The degrading images of blackness that emerged from racist white imagination and that were circulated widely in the dominant culture (on salt shakers, cookie jars, pancake boxes) could be countered by "true-to-life" images. When the psychohistory of a people is marked by ongoing loss, when entire histories are denied, hidden, erased, documentation can become an obsession. The camera must have seemed a magical instrument to many of the displaced and marginalized groups trying to carve out new destinies for themselves in the Americas. More than any other image-making tool, the camera offered African-Americans, disempowered in white culture, a way to empower ourselves through representation. For black folks, the camera provided a means to document a reality that could, if necessary, be packed, stored, moved from place to place. It was documentation that could be shared, passed around. And, ultimately, these images, the world they recorded, could be hidden, to be discovered at another time. Had the camera been there when slavery ended, it could have provided images that would have helped folks searching for lost kin and loved ones. It would have been a powerful tool of cultural recovery. Half a century later, the generations of black folks emerging from a history of loss became passionately obsessed with the camera. Elderly black people developed a cultural passion for the camera, for the images it produced, because it offered a way to contain memories, to overcome loss, to keep history.

Though rarely articulated as such, the camera became in black life a political instrument, a way to resist misrepresentation as well as a means by which alternative images could be produced. Photography was more fascinating to masses of black folks than other forms of image making because it offered the possibility of immediate intervention, useful in the production of counterhegemonic representations even as it was also an instrument of pleasure. The camera allowed black folks to combine image making, resistance struggle, and pleasure. Taking pictures was fun!

Growing up in the 1950s, I was somewhat awed and at times frightened by our extended family's emphasis on picture taking. From the images of the dead as they lay serene, beautiful, and still in open caskets to the endless portraits of newborns, every wall and corner of my grandparents' (and most everybody else's) home was lined with photographs. When I was young I never linked this obsession with self-representation to our history as a domestically colonized and subjugated people.

My perspective on picture taking was also informed by the way the process was tied to patriarchy in our household. Our father was definitely the "picture-takin' man." For a long time cameras remained mysterious and off limits to the rest of us. As the only one in the family who had access to the equipment, who could learn how to make the process work, my father exerted control over our images. In charge of capturing our family history with the camera, he called and took the shots. We were constantly being lined up for picture taking, and it was years before our household could experience this as an enjoyable activity,

before any of the rest of us could be behind the camera. Until then, picture taking was serious business. I hated it. I hated posing. I hated cameras. I hated the images that cameras produced. When I stopped living at home, I refused to be captured by anyone's camera. I did not wish to document my life, the changes, the presence of different places, people, and so on. I wanted to leave no trace. I wanted there to be no walls in my life that would, like gigantic maps, chart my journey. I wanted to stand outside history.

That was twenty years ago. Now that I am passionately involved with thinking critically about black people and representation, I can confess that those walls of photographs empowered me, and that I feel their absence in my life. Right now I long for those walls, those curatorial spaces in the home that express our will to make and display images.

Sarah Oldham, my mother's mother, was a keeper of walls. Throughout my childhood, visits to her house were like trips to a gallery or museum—experiences we did not have because of racial segregation. We would stand before the walls of images and learn the importance of the arrangement, why a certain photograph was placed here and not there. The walls were fundamentally different from photo albums. Rather than shutting images away, where they could be seen only upon request, the walls were a public announcement of the primacy of the image, the joy of image making. To enter black homes in my childhood was to enter a world that valued the visual, that asserted our collective will to participate in a noninstitutionalized curatorial process.

For black folks constructing our identities within the culture of apartheid, these walls were essential to the process of decolonization. In opposition to colonizing socialization, internalized racism, these walls announced our visual complexity. We saw ourselves represented in these images not as caricatures, cartoonlike figures; we were there in full diversity of body, being, and expression, multidimensional. Reflecting the way black folks looked at themselves in those private spaces, where those ways of looking were not being overseen by a white colonizing eye, a white-supremacist gaze, these images created ruptures in our experience of the visual. They challenged both white perceptions of blackness and that realm of black-produced image making that reflected internalized racism. Many of these images demanded that we look at ourselves with new eyes, that we create oppositional standards of evaluation. As we looked at black skin in snapshots, the techniques for lightening skin that professional photographers often used when shooting black images were suddenly exposed as a colonizing aesthetic. Photographs taken in everyday life, snapshots in particular, rebelled against all those photographic practices that reinscribed colonial ways of looking and capturing the images of the black "other." Shot spontaneously, without any notion of remaking black bodies in the image of whiteness, snapshots posed a challenge to black viewers. Unlike photographs constructed so that black images would appear as the embodiment of colonizing fantasies, snapshots gave us a way to see ourselves, a sense of how we looked when we were not "wearing the mask," when we were not attempting to perfect the image for a white-supremacist gaze.

Although most black folks did not articulate their desire to look at images of themselves that did not resemble or please white folks' ideas about us, or that did not frame us within an image of racial hierarchies, that desire was expressed through our passionate engagement with informal photographic practices. Creating pictorial genealogies was the means by which one could ensure against the losses of the past. Such genealogies were a way to sustain ties. As children, we learned who our ancestors were by listening to endless narratives as we stood in front of these pictures.

In many black homes, photographs—especially snapshots—were also central to the creation of "altars." These commemorative places paid homage to absent loved ones. Snapshots or professional portraits were placed in specific settings so that a relationship with the dead could be continued. Poignantly describing this use of the image in her novel Jazz, Toni Morrison writes:

> ...a dead girl's face has become a
> necessary thing for their nights. They
> each take turns to throw off the bedcov-
> ers, rise up from the sagging mattress
> and tiptoe over cold linoleum into the
> parlor to gaze at what seems like the

only living presence in the house:
the photograph of a bold, unsmiling
girl staring from the mantelpiece.
If the tiptoer is Joe Trace, driven by
loneliness from his wife's side, then
the face stares at him without hope
or regret and it is the absence of
accusation that wakes him from his
sleep hungry for her company. No finger
points. Her lips don't turn down in
judgment. Her face is calm, gener-
ous and sweet. But if the tiptoer is
Violet, the photograph is not that
at all. The girl's face looks greedy,
haughty and very lazy. The cream-at-
the-top-of-the-milkpail face of someone who will never work for anything,
someone who picks up things lying on
other people's dressers and is not
embarrassed when found out. It is the
face of a sneak who glides over to your
sink to rinse the fork you have laid by
your place. An inward face—whatever
it sees is its own self. You are there,
it says, because I am looking at you.

I quote this passage at length because it attests to a kind of connection to photographic images that has not been acknowledged in critical discussions of black folks' relationship to the visual. When I first read these sentences, I was reminded of the passionate way we related to photographs when I was a child. Fictively dramatizing the extent to which a photograph can have a "living presence," Morrison describes the way that many black folks rooted in Southern tradition once used, and still use, pictures. They were and remain a mediation between the living and the dead.

To create a palimpsest of black folks' relation to the visual in segregated black life, we need to follow each trace, not fall into the trap of thinking that if something was not openly discussed, or only talked about and not recorded, it lacks significance and meaning. Those pictorial genealogies that Sarah Oldham, my mother's mother, constructed on her walls were essential to our sense of self and identity as a family.

They provided a necessary narrative, a way for us to enter history without words. When words entered, they did so in order to make the images live. Many older black folks who cherished pictures were not literate. The images were crucial documentation, there to sustain and affirm memory. This was true for my grandmother, who did not read or write. I focus especially on her walls because I know that, as an artist (she was an excellent quiltmaker), she positioned the photos with the same care that she laid our her quilts.

The walls of pictures were indeed maps guiding us through diverse journeys. Seeking to recover strands of oppositional worldviews that were a part of black folks' historical relationship to the visual, to the process of image making, many black folks are once again looking to photography to make the connection. The contemporary African-American artist Emma Amos maps our journeys when she mixes photographs with painting, making connections between past and present. Amos uses snapshots inherited from an uncle who once took pictures for a living. In one piece, Amos paints a map of the United States and identifies diasporic African presences, as well as particular Native American communities with black kin, marking each spot with a family image.

Drawing from the past, from those walls of images I grew up with, I gather snapshots and lay them out to see what narratives the images tell, what they say without words. I search these images to see if there are imprints waiting to be seen, recognized, and read. Together, a black male friend and I lay out the snapshots of his boyhood to see when he began to lose a certain openness, to discern at what age he began to shut down, to close himself away. Through these images, my friend hopes to find a way back to the self he once was. We are awed by what our snapshots reveal, what they enable us to remember.

The word *remember* (*re-member*) evokes the coming together of severed parts, fragments becoming a whole. Photography has been, and is, central to that aspect of decolonization that calls us back to the past and offers a way to reclaim and renew life-affirming bonds. Using images, we connect ourselves to a recuperative, redemptive memory that enables us to construct radical identities, images of ourselves that transcend the limits of the colonizing eye.

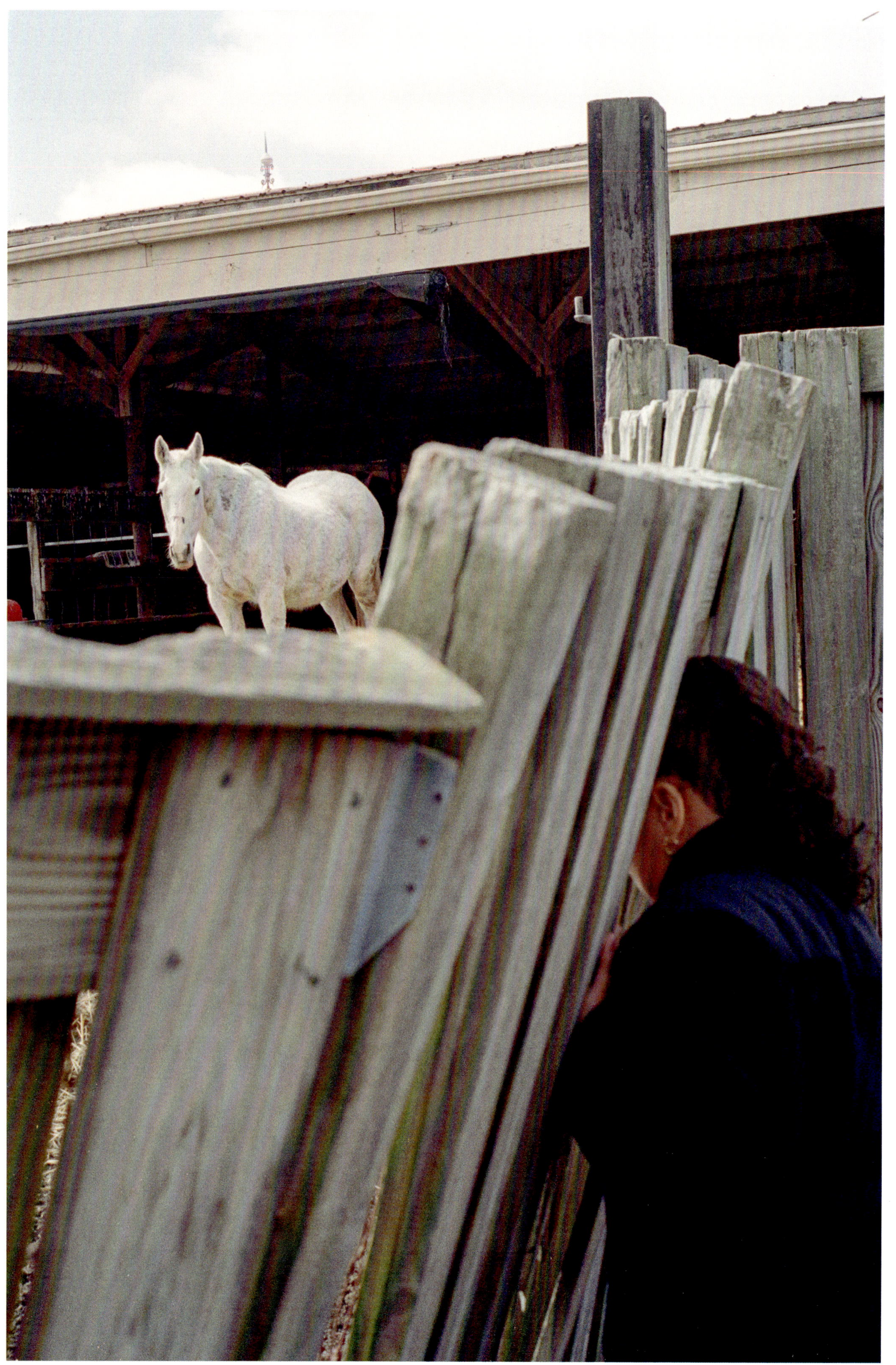

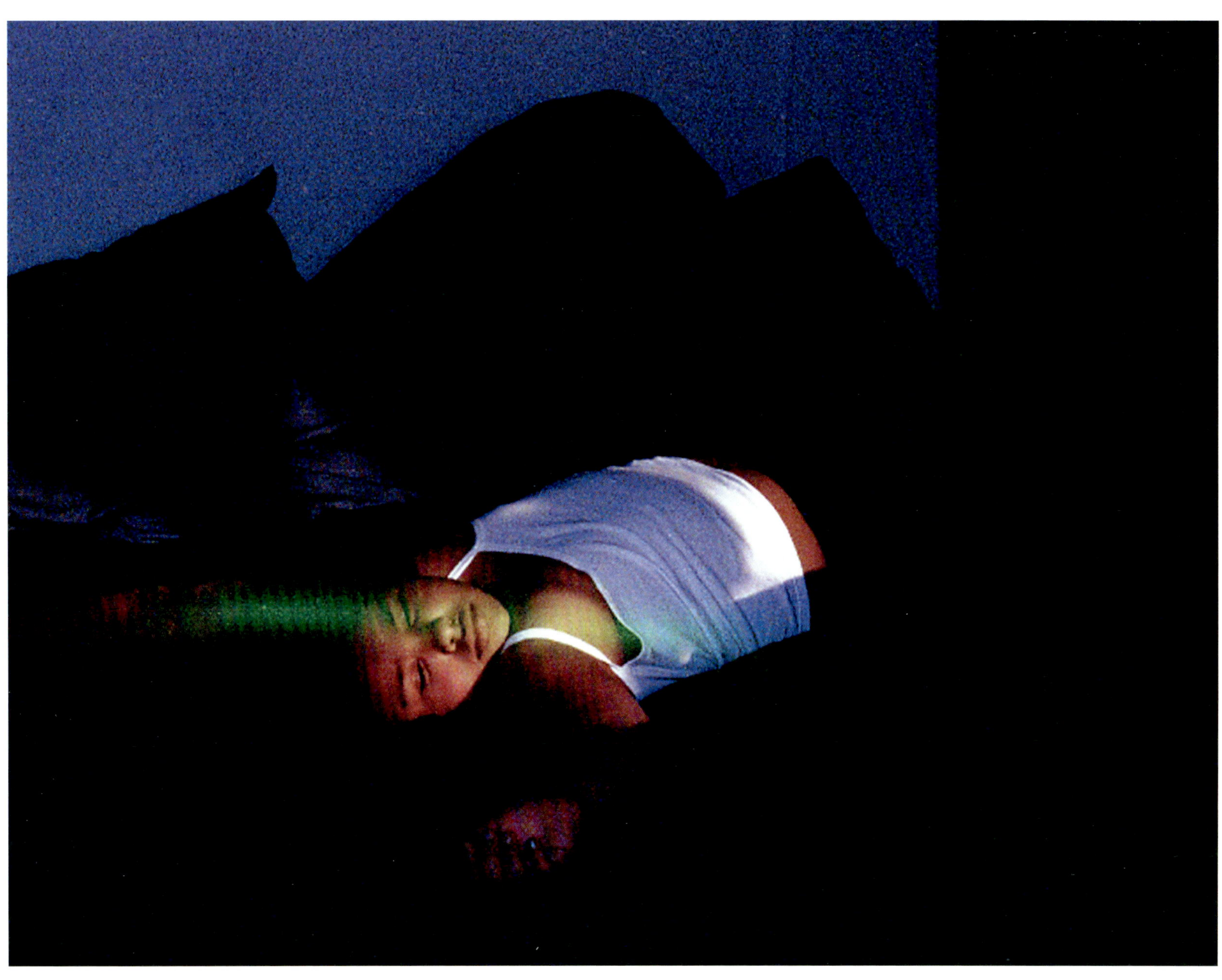

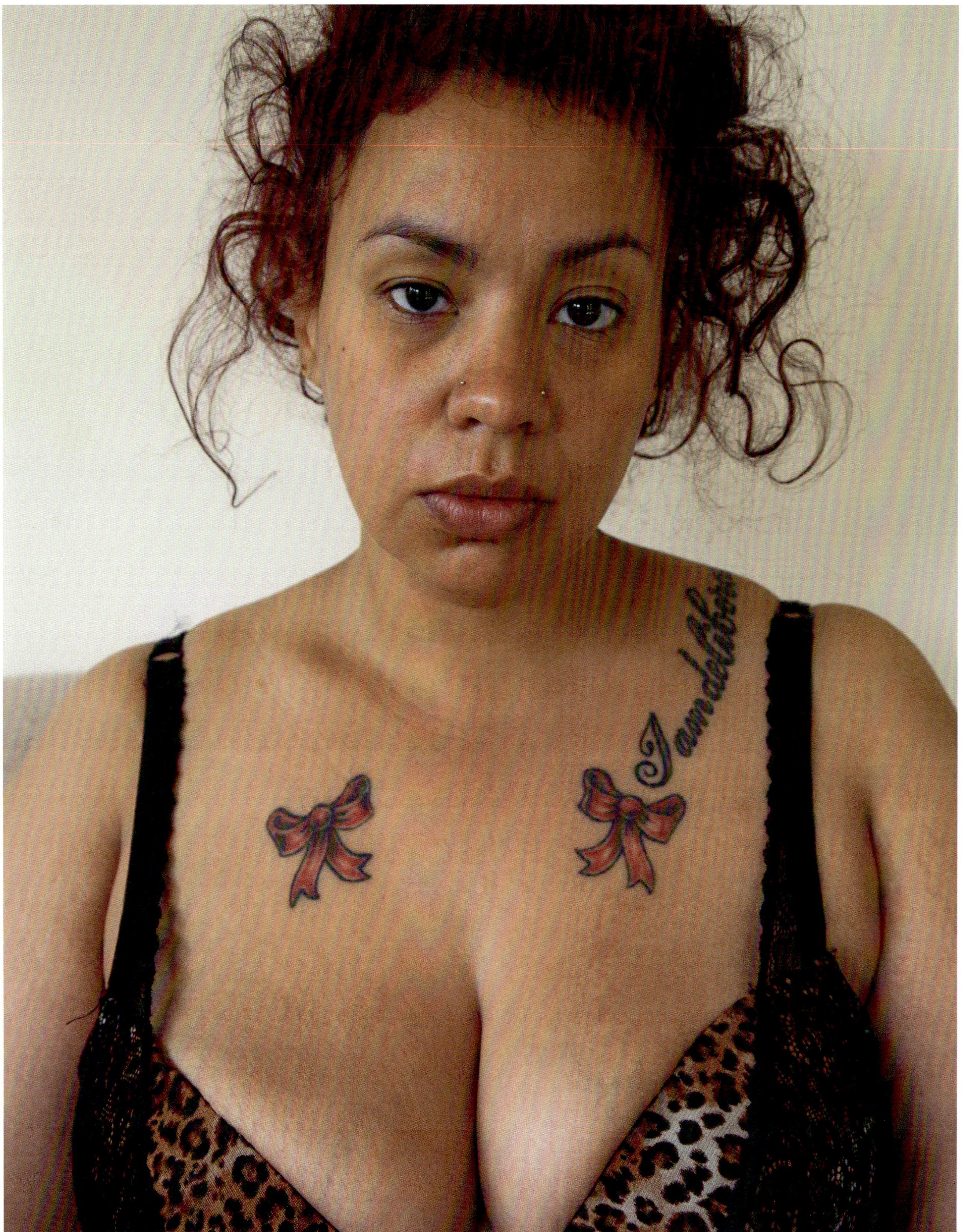

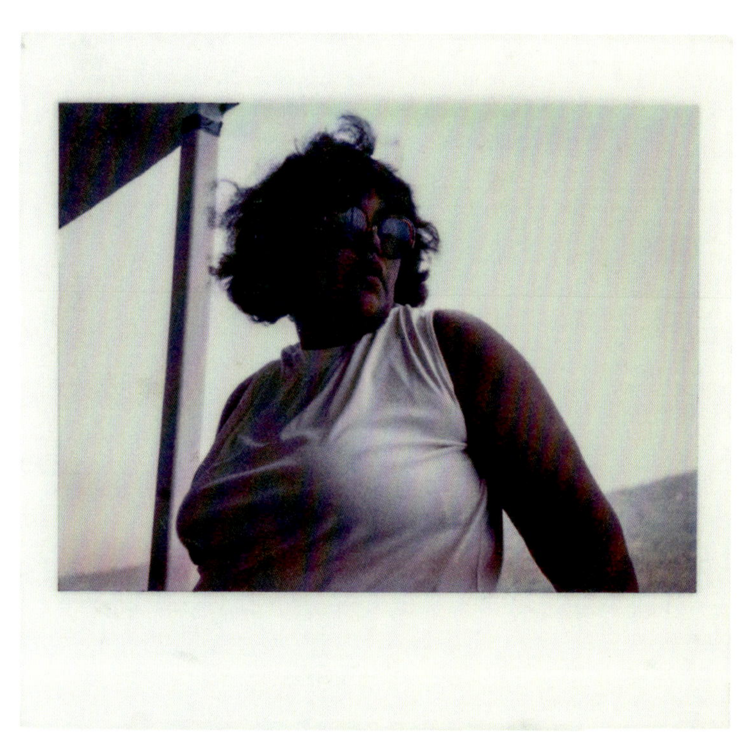

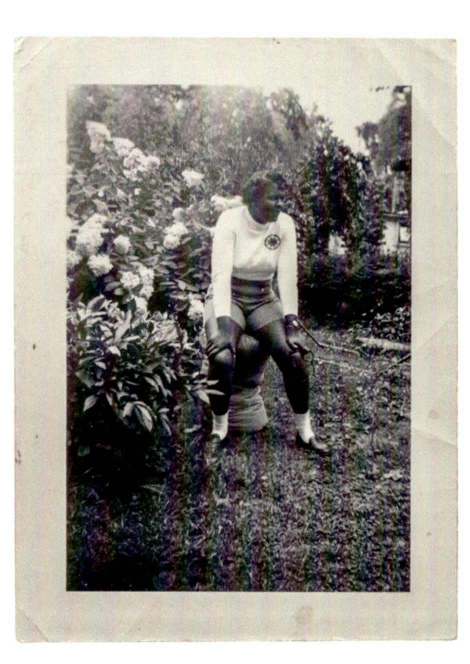

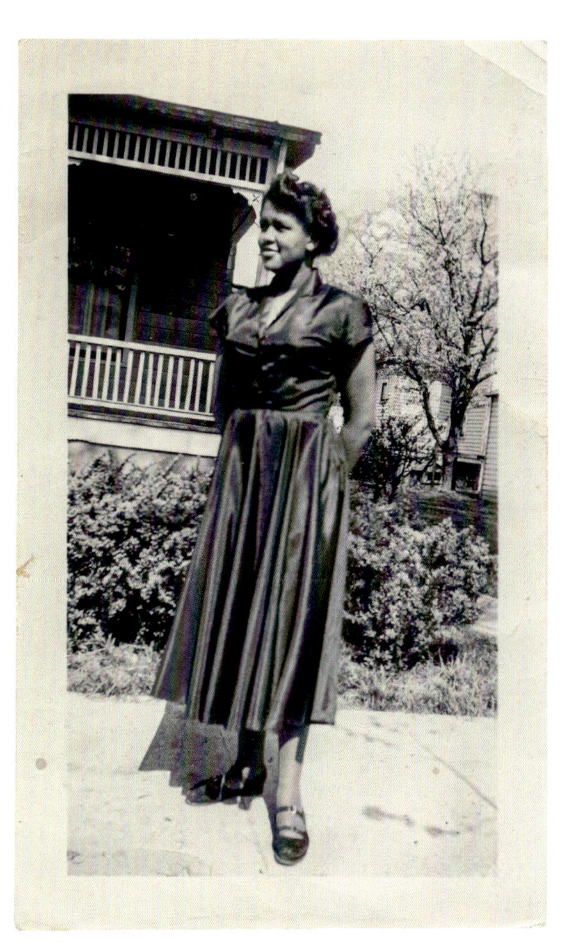

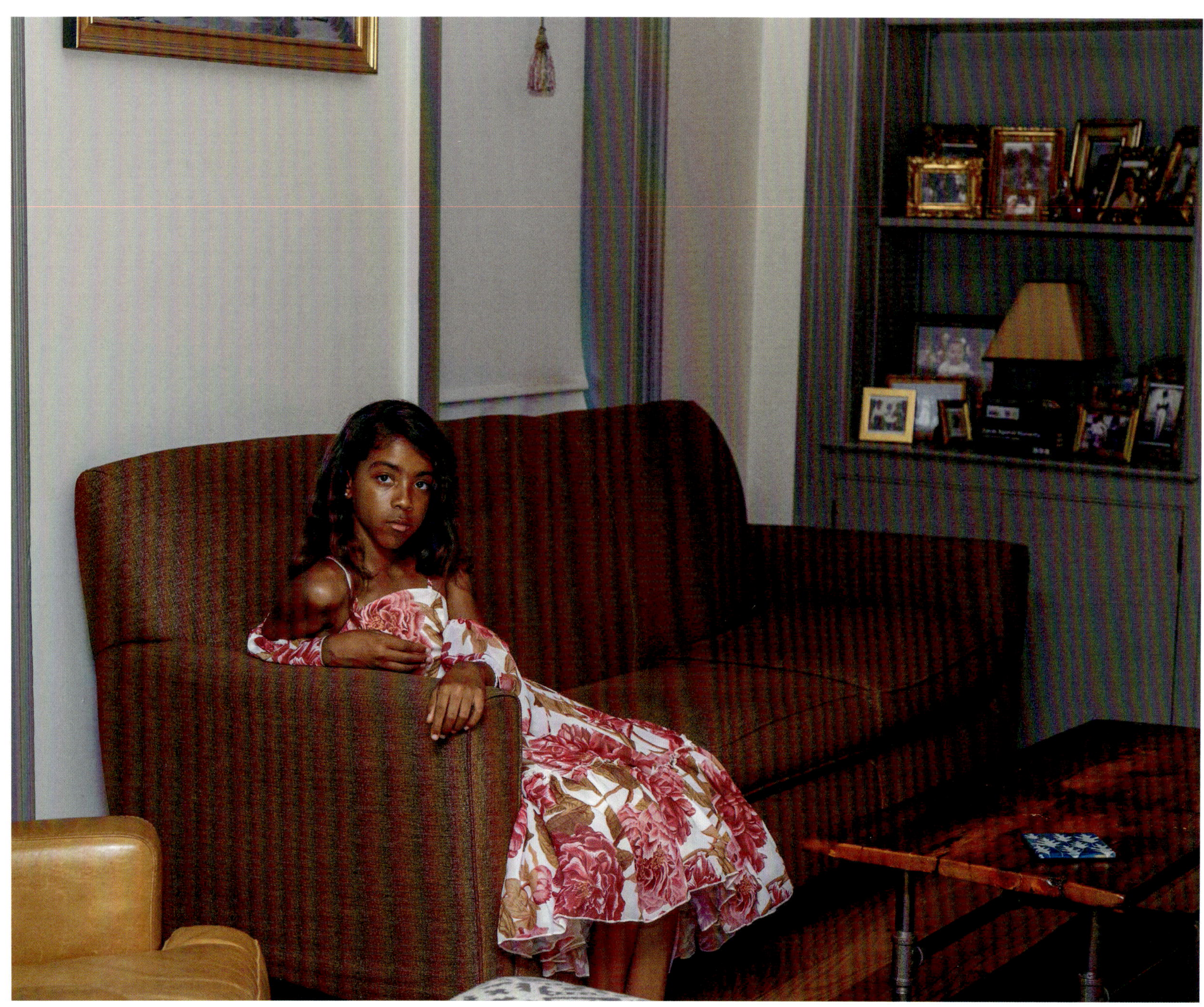

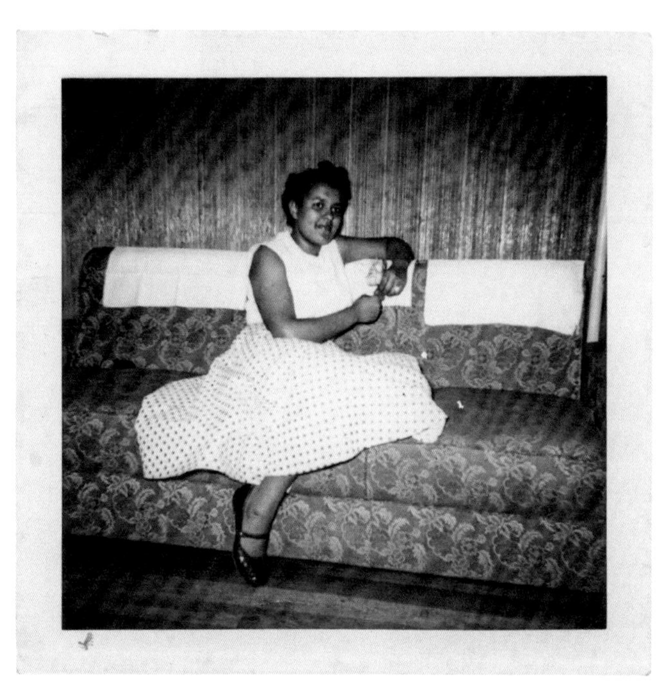

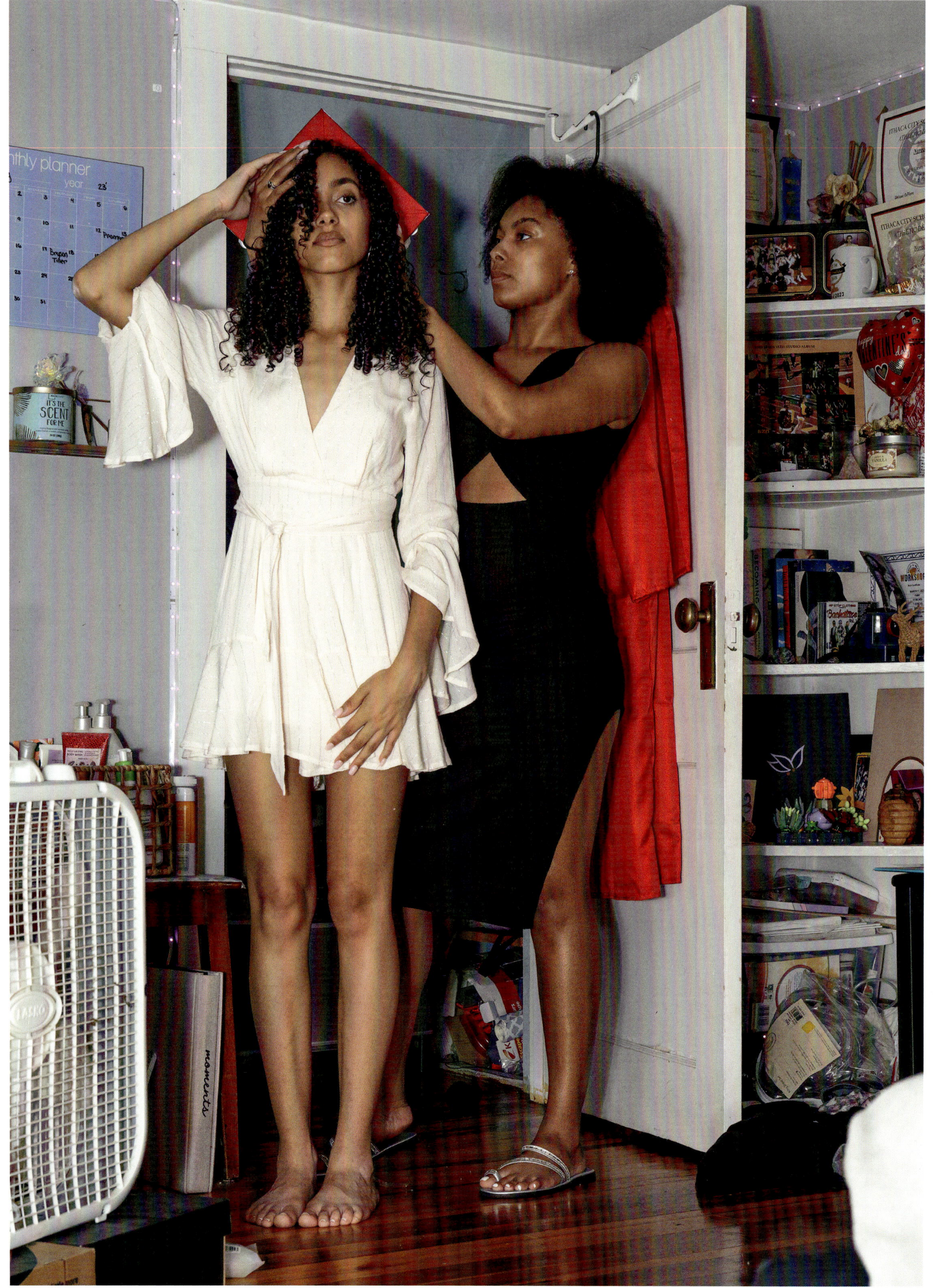

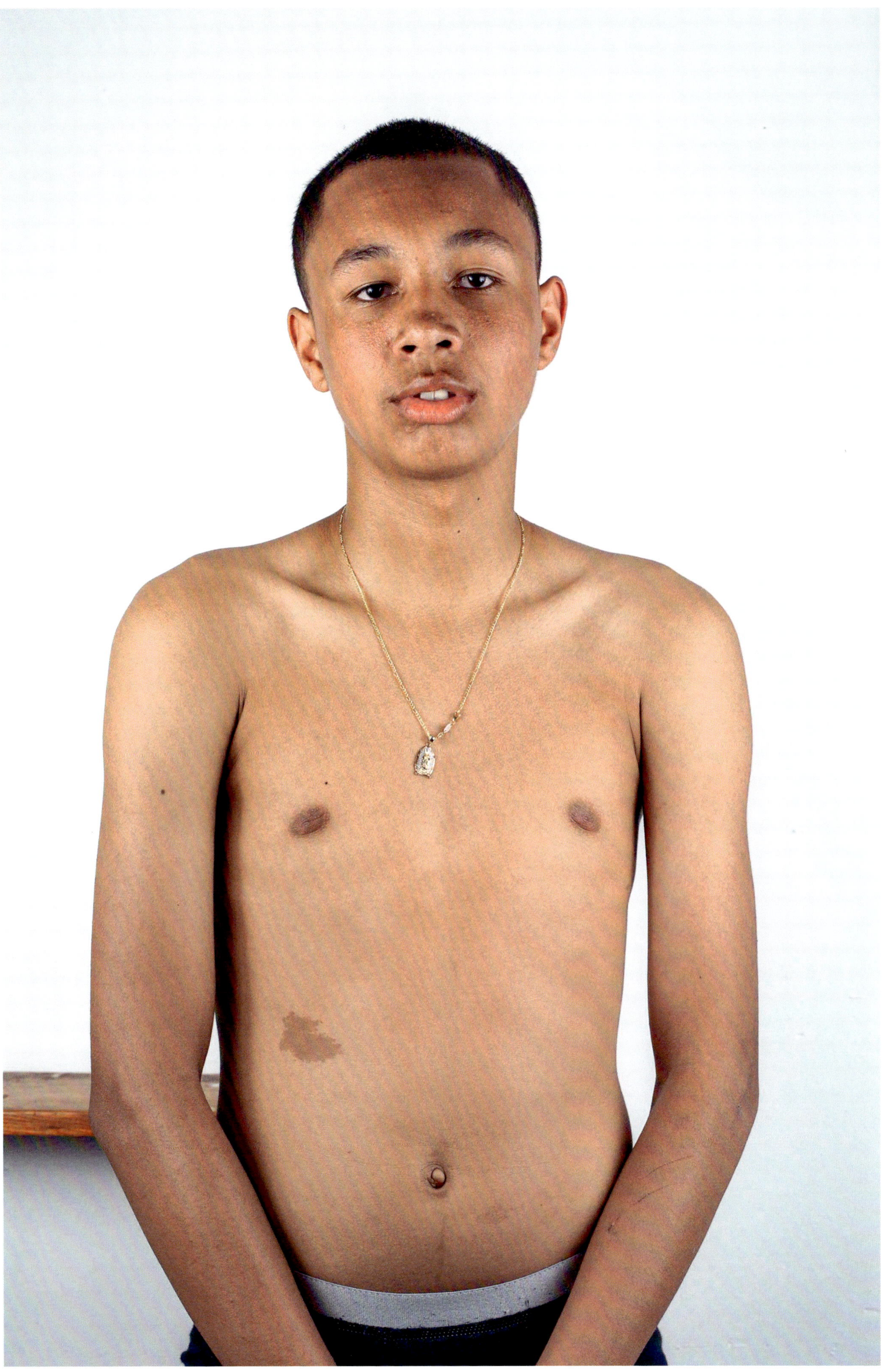

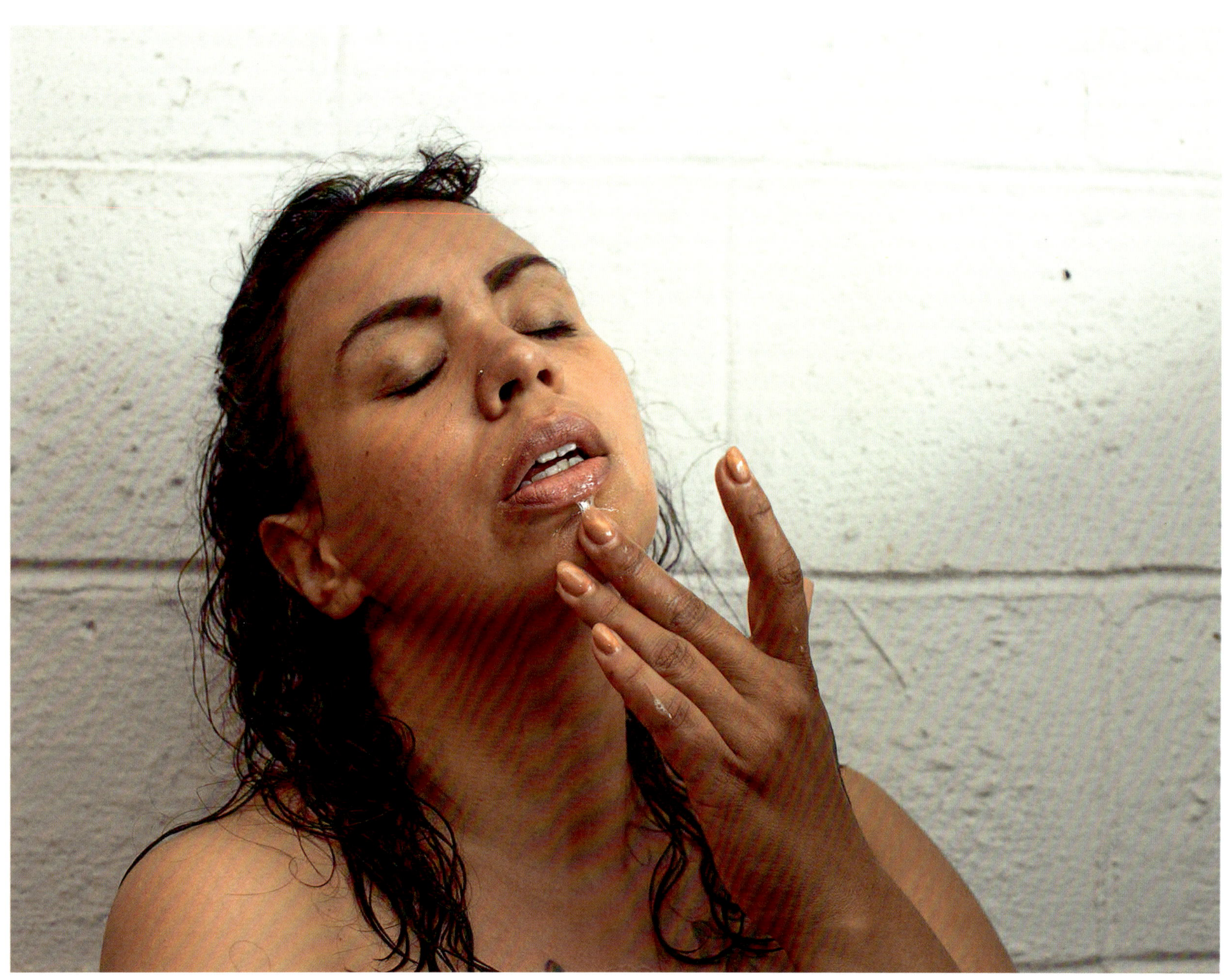

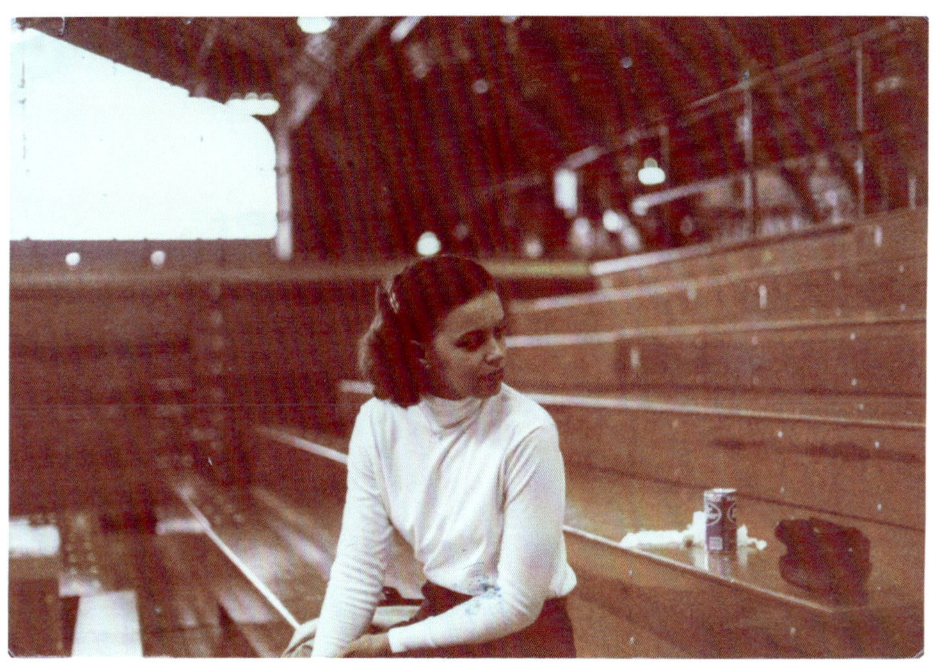

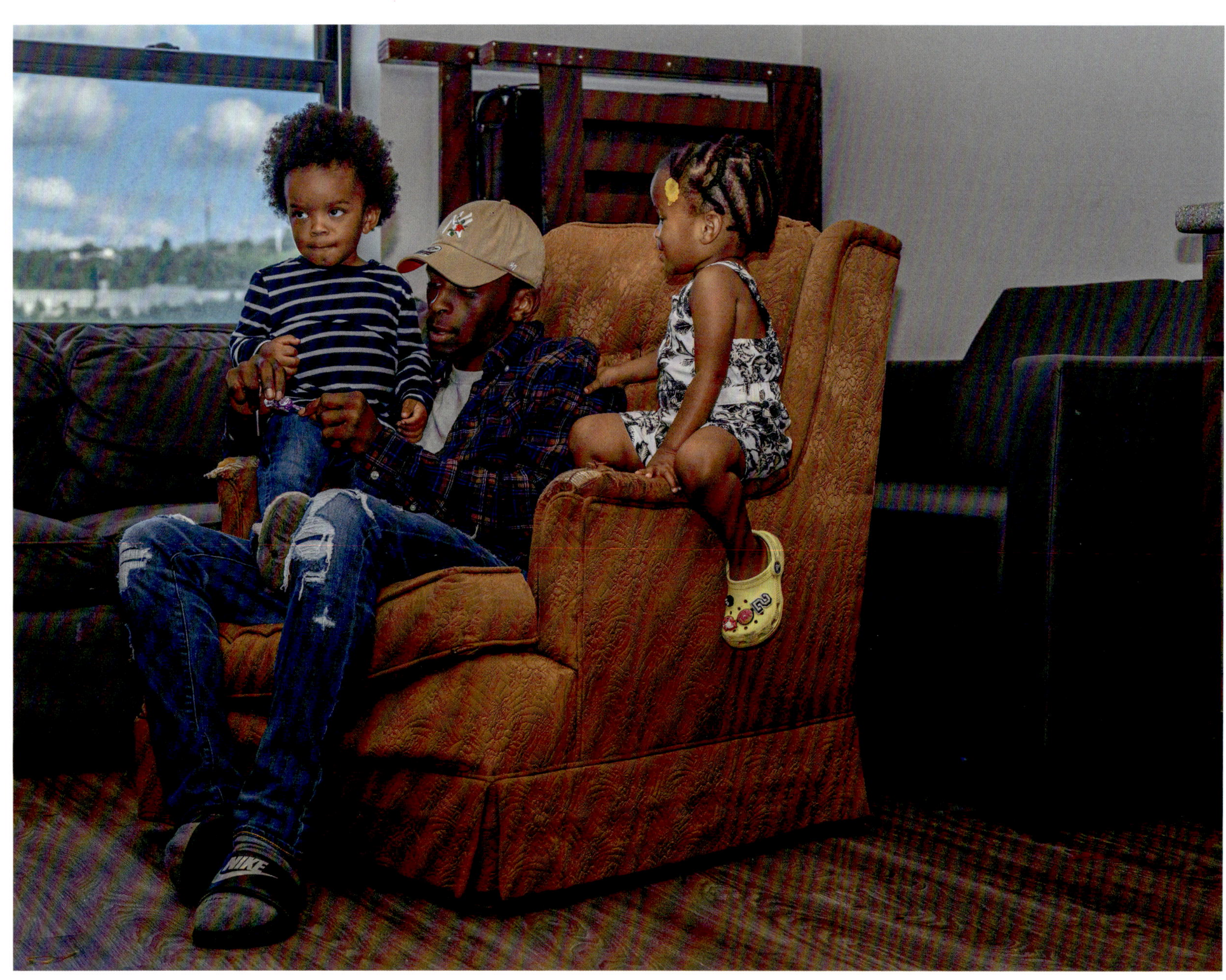

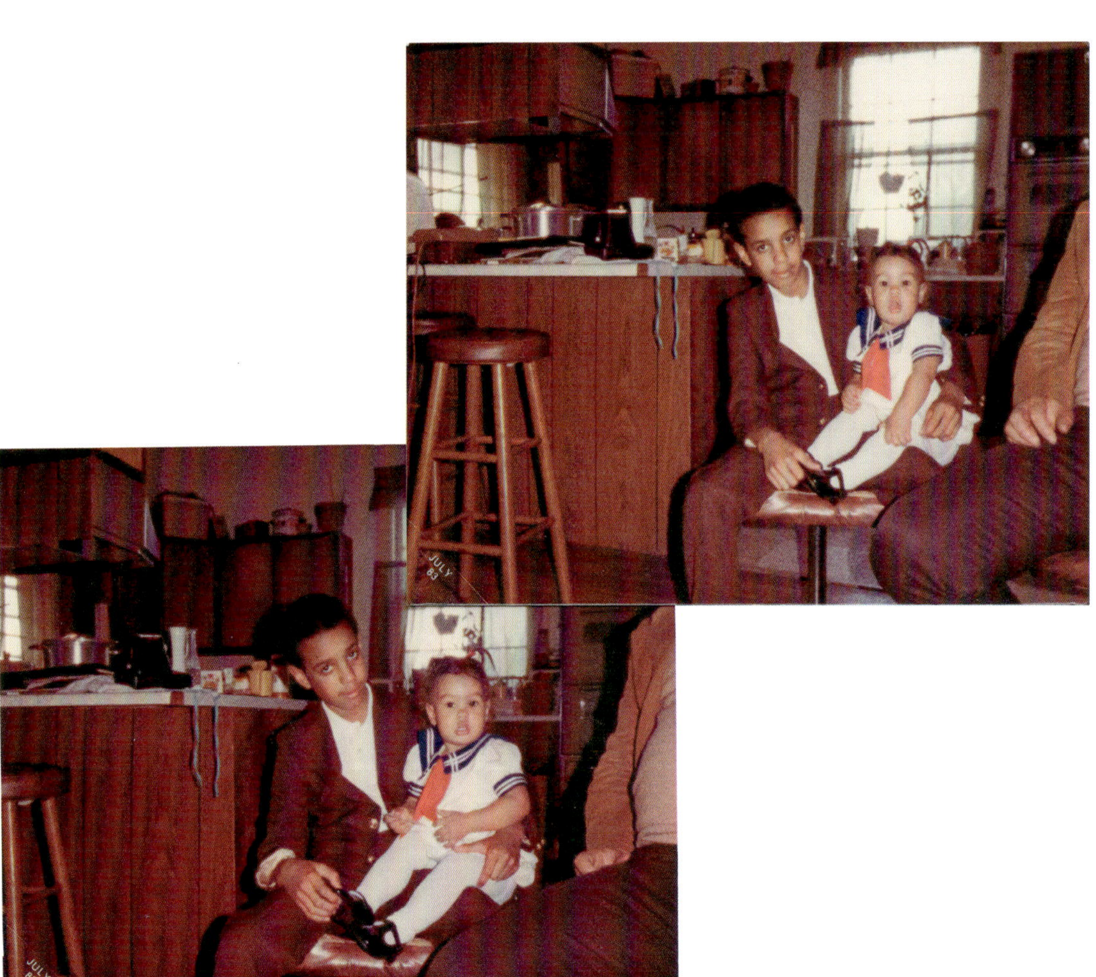

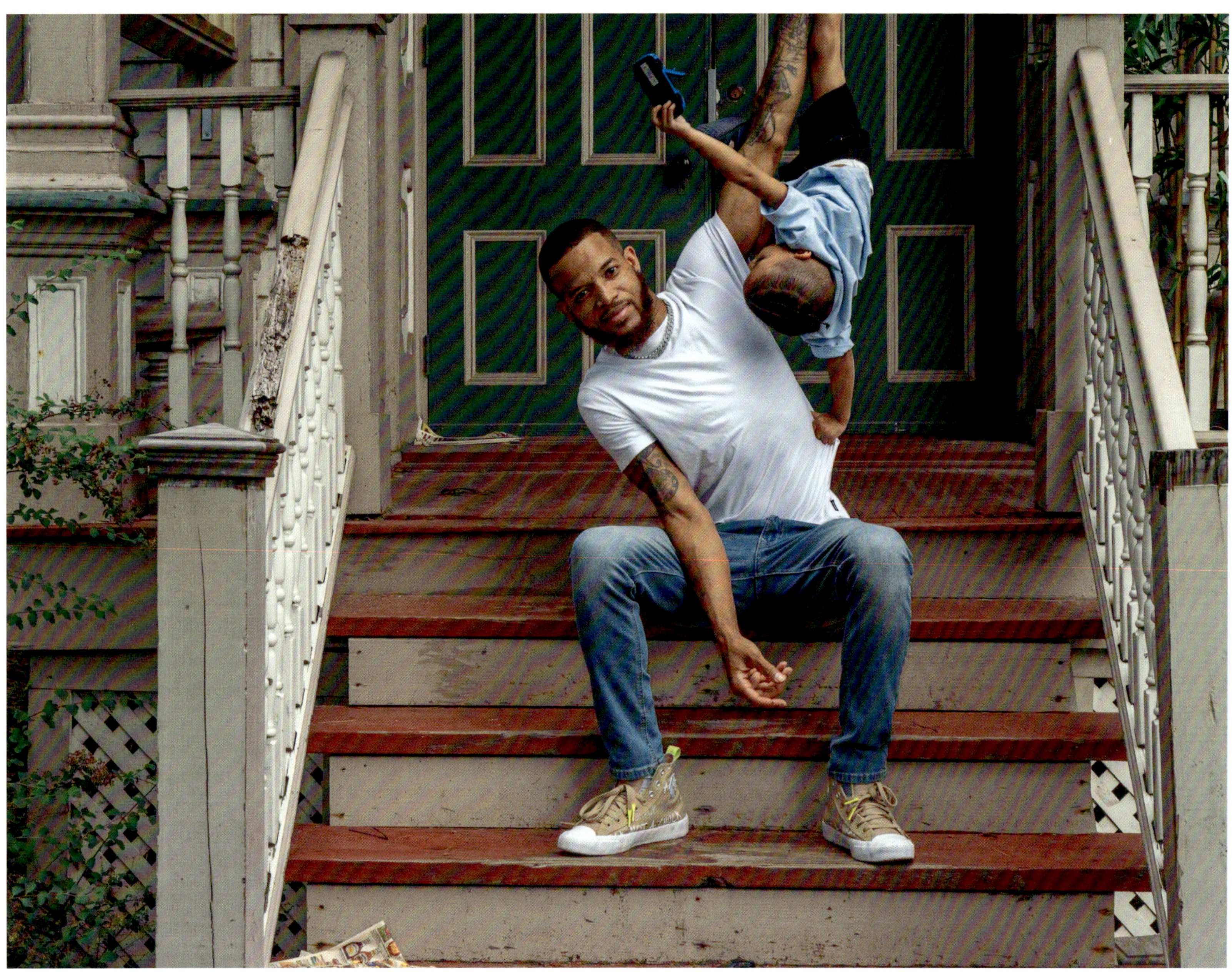

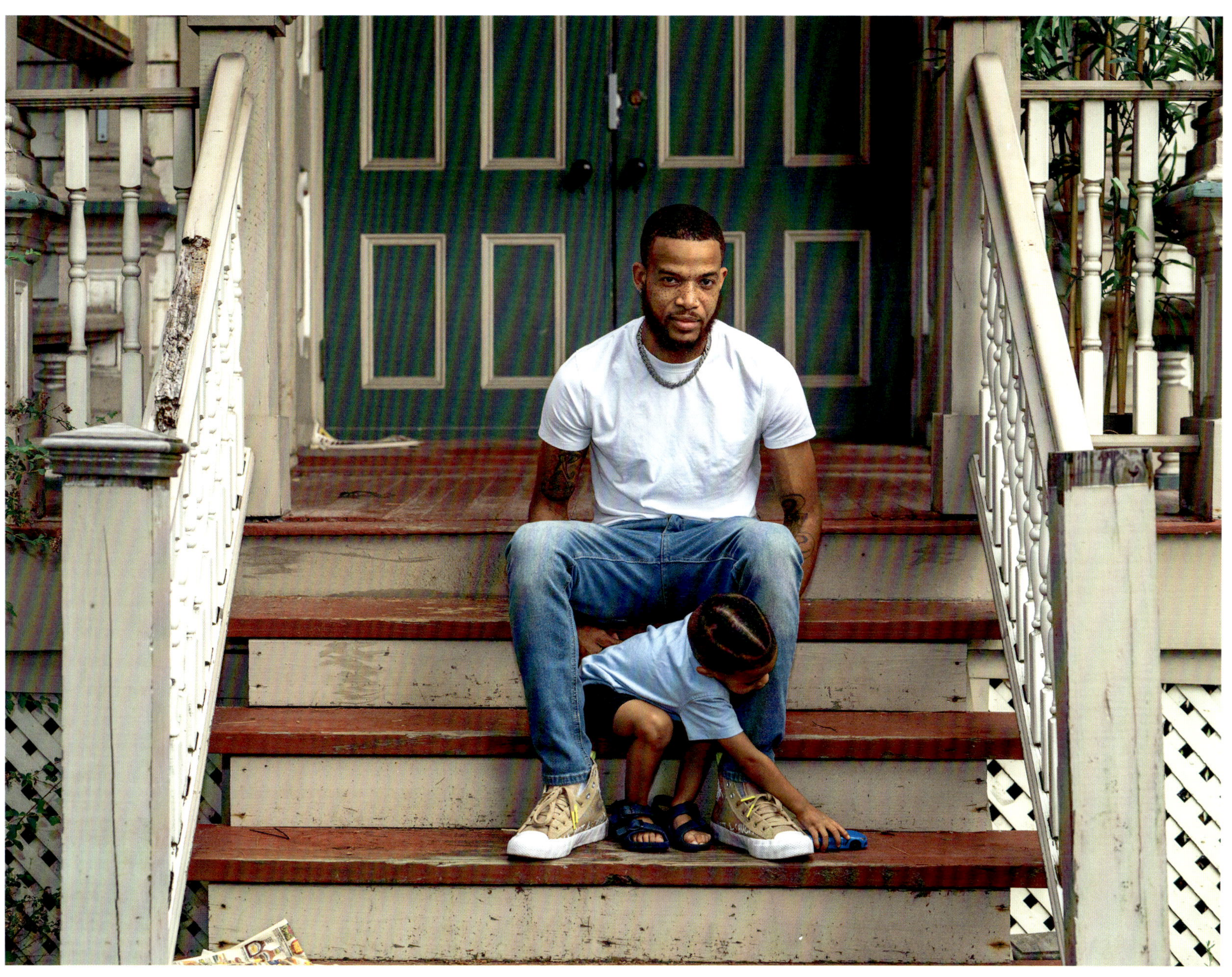

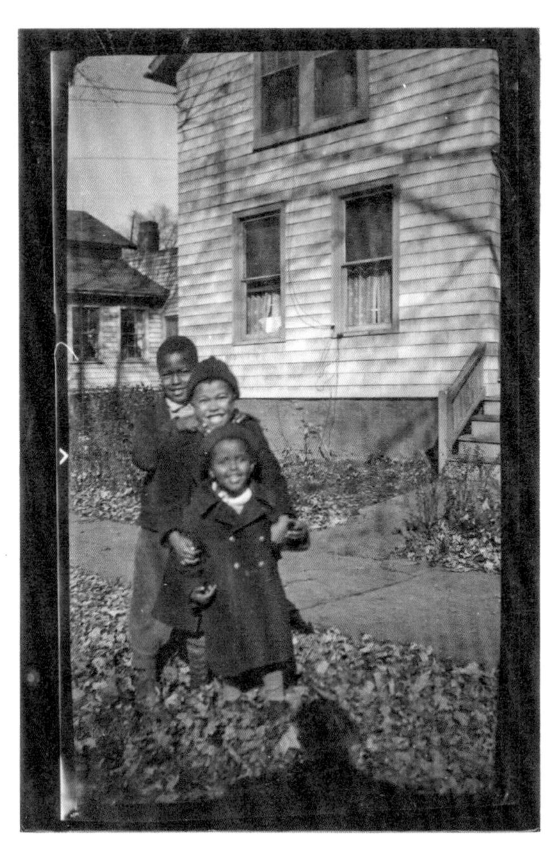

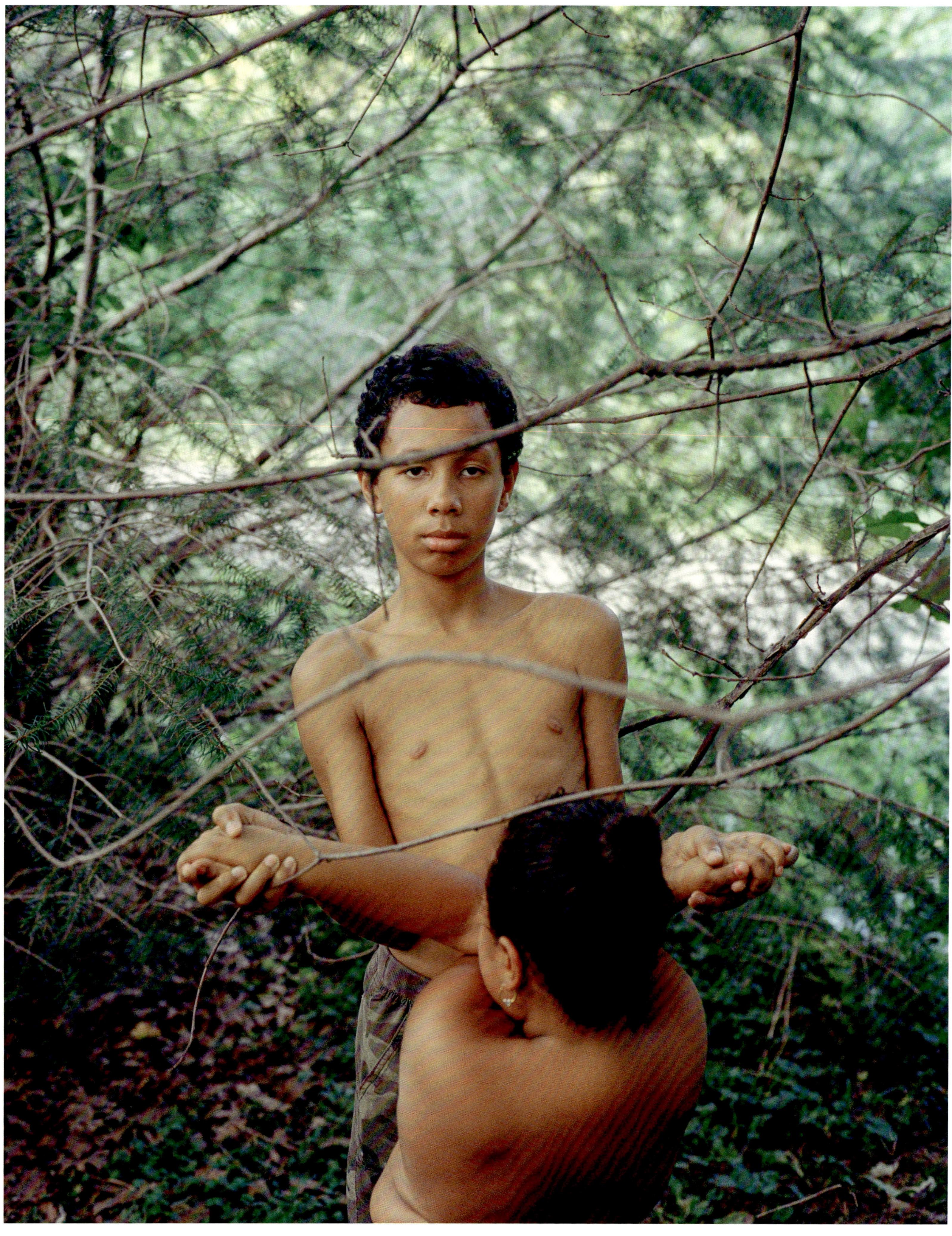

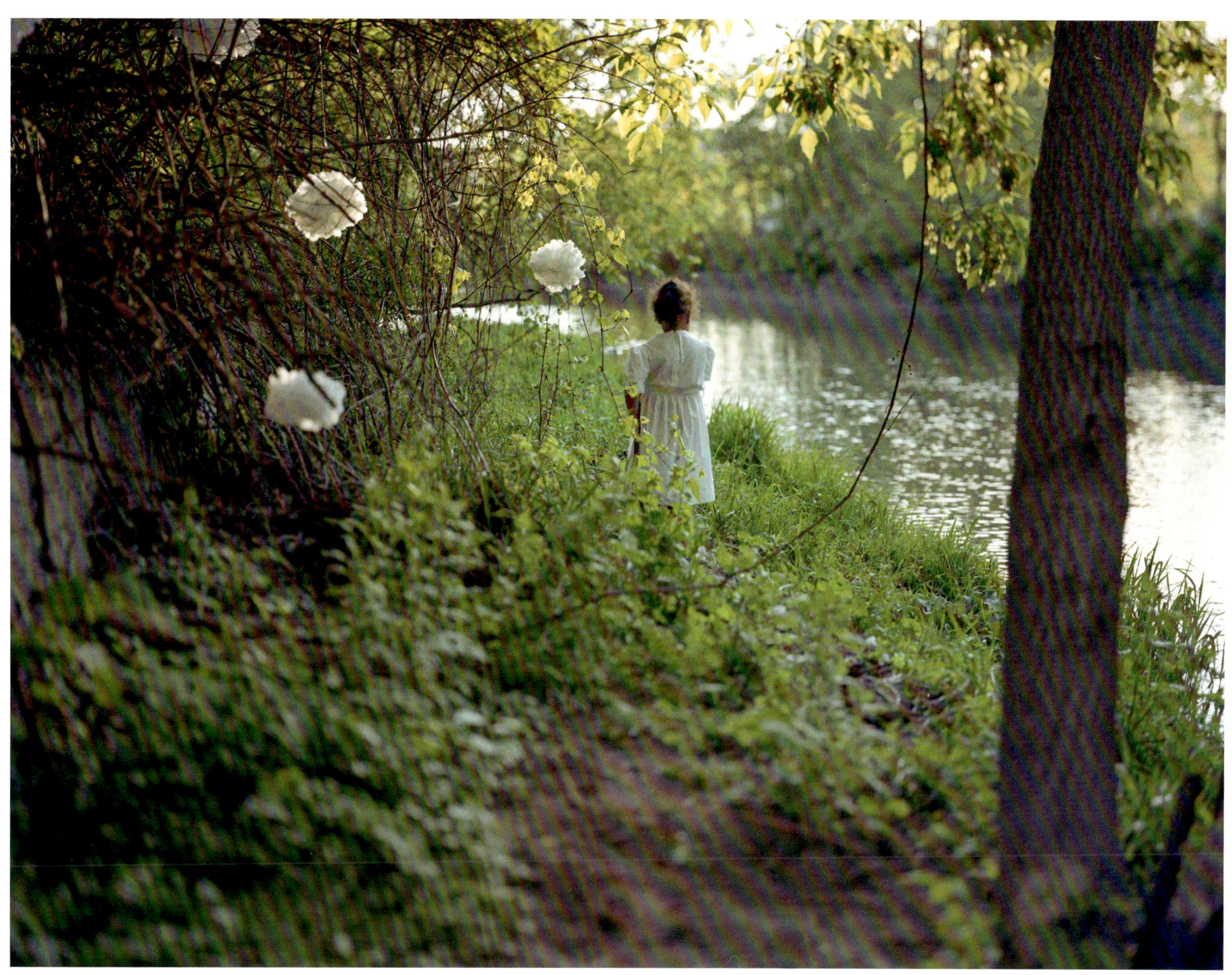

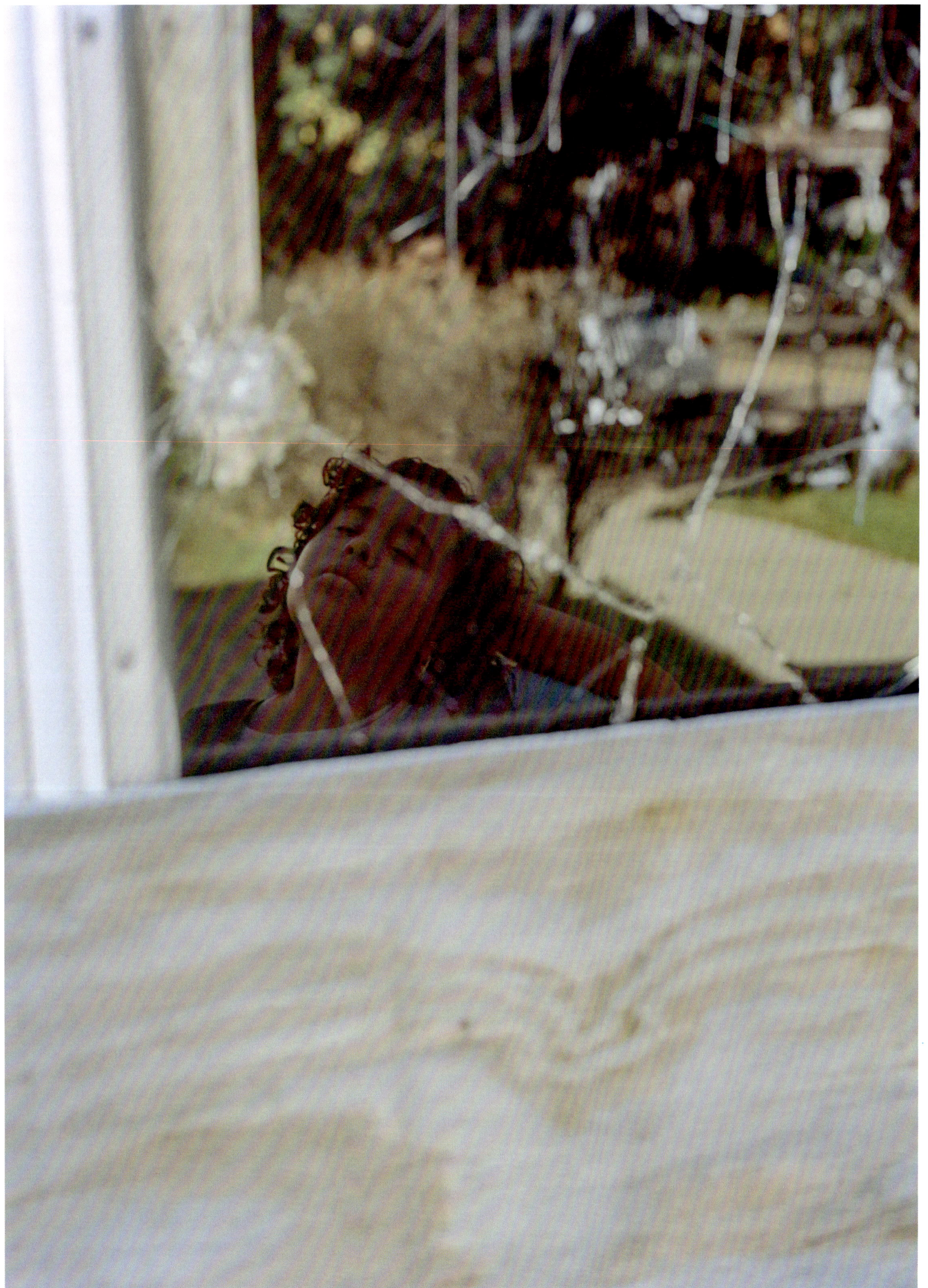

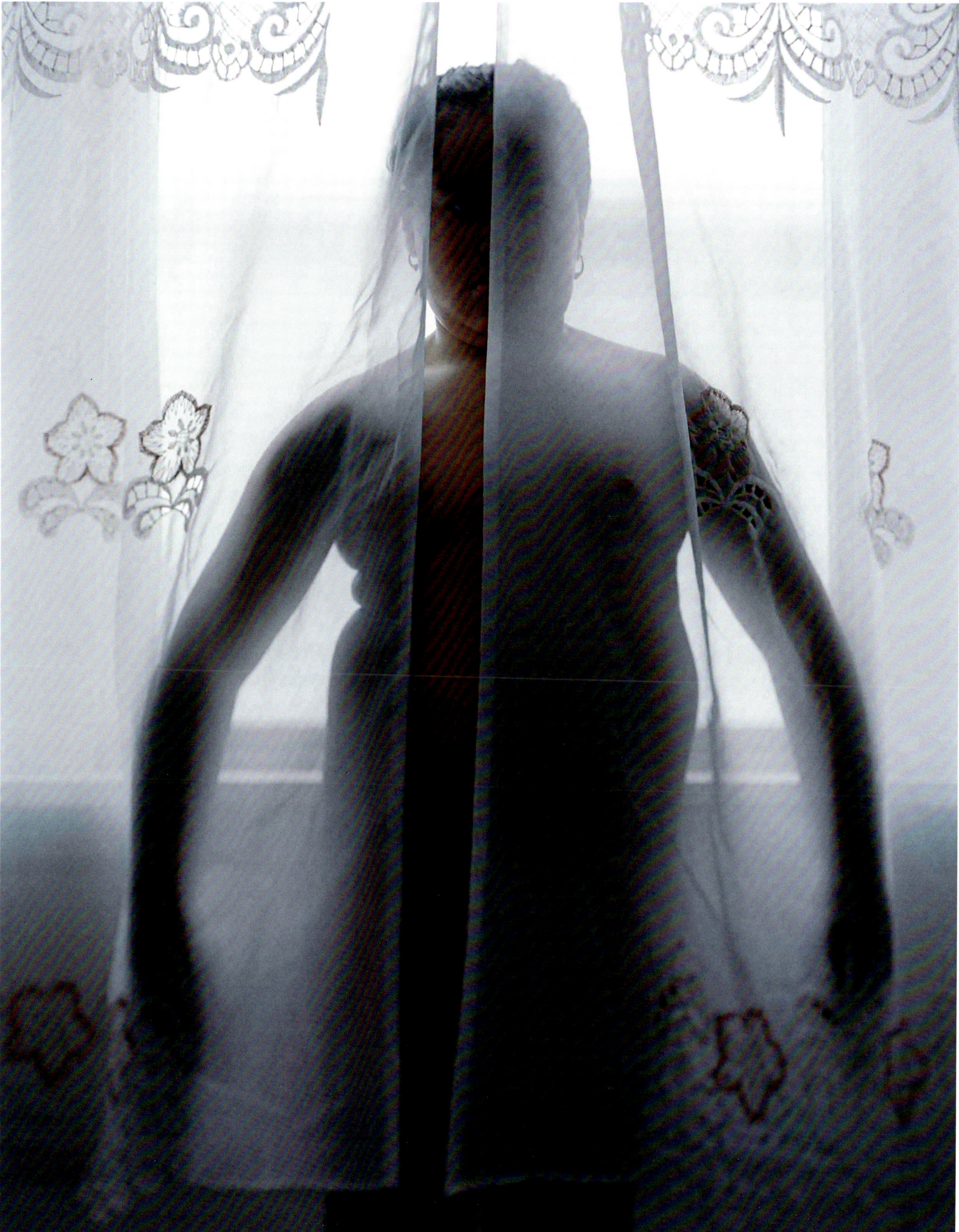

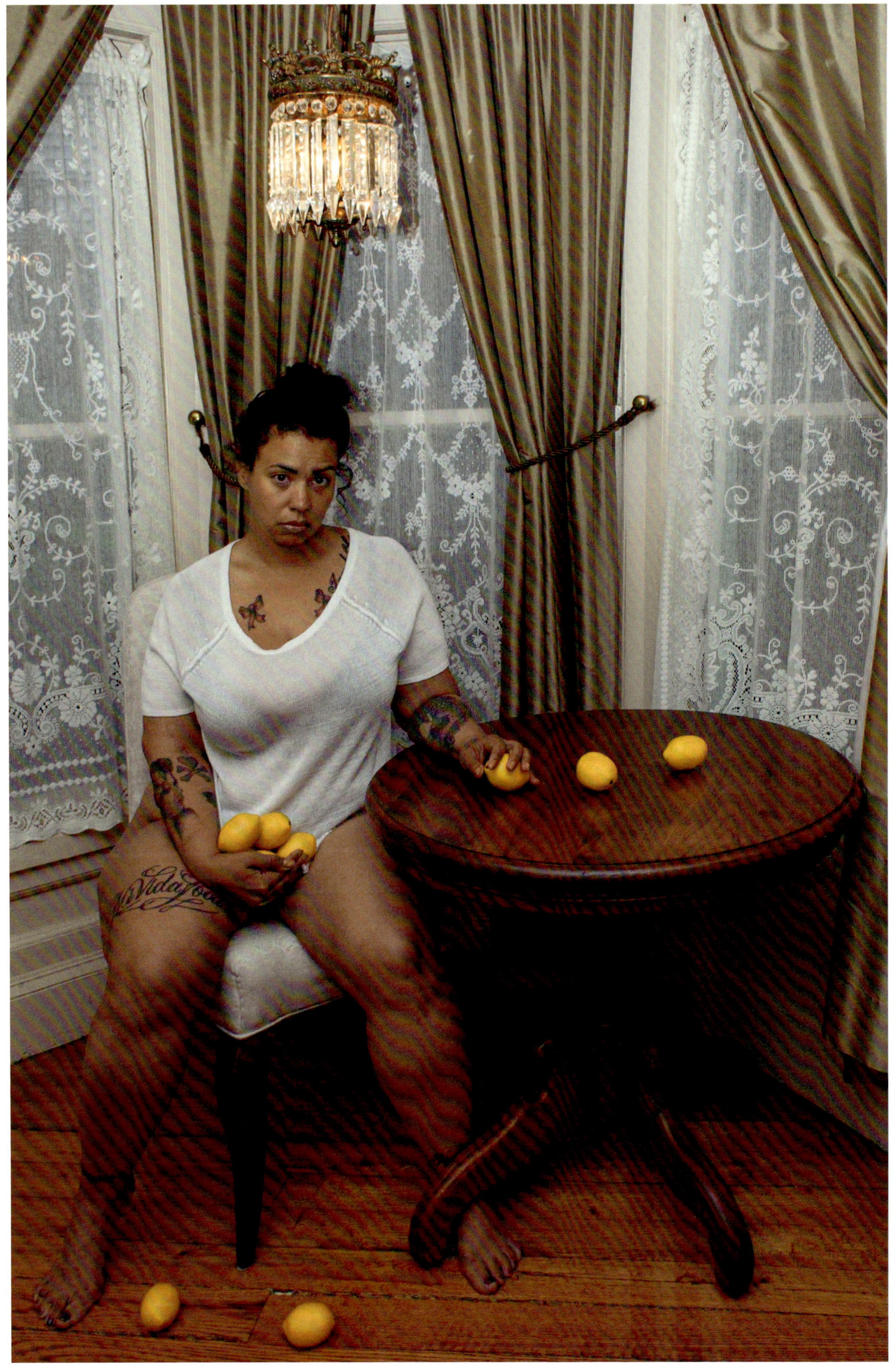

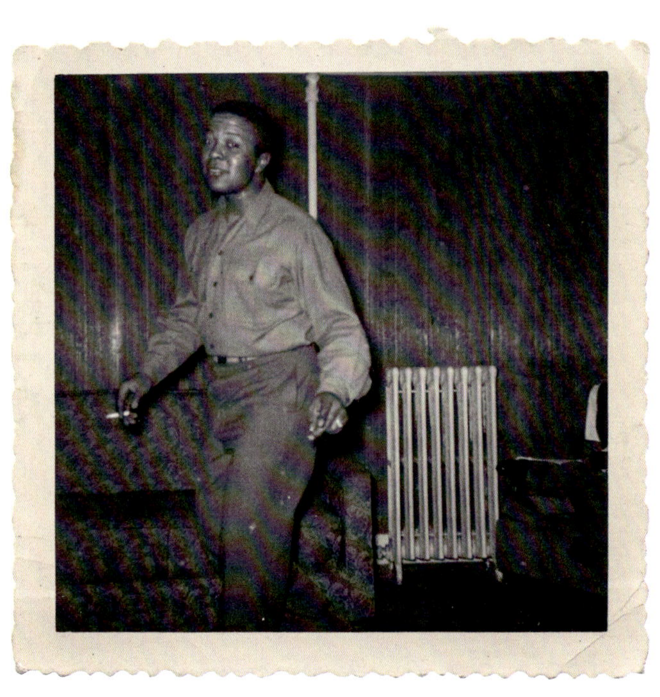

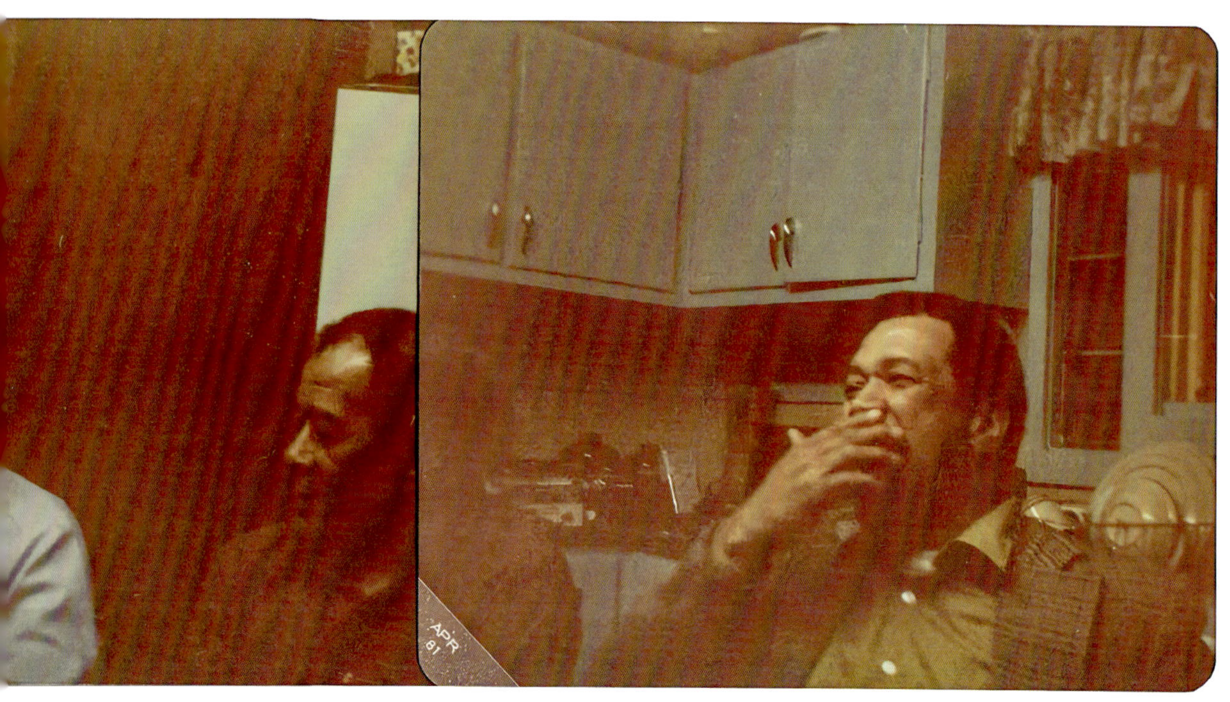

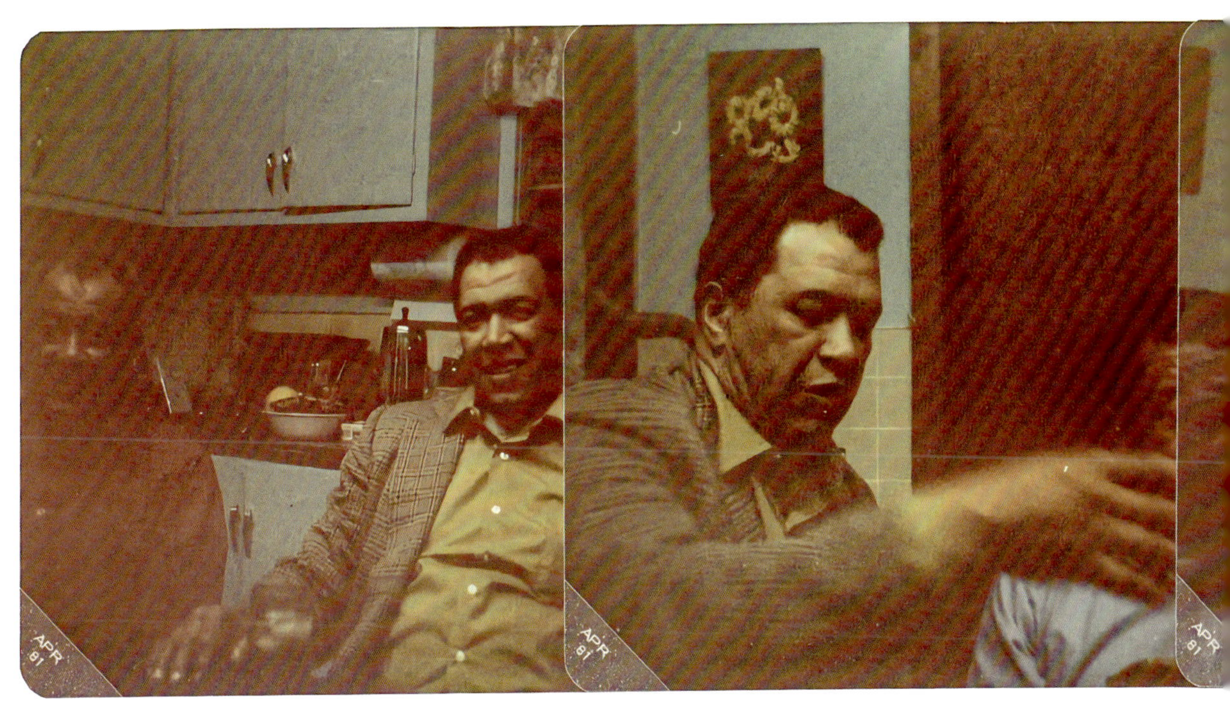

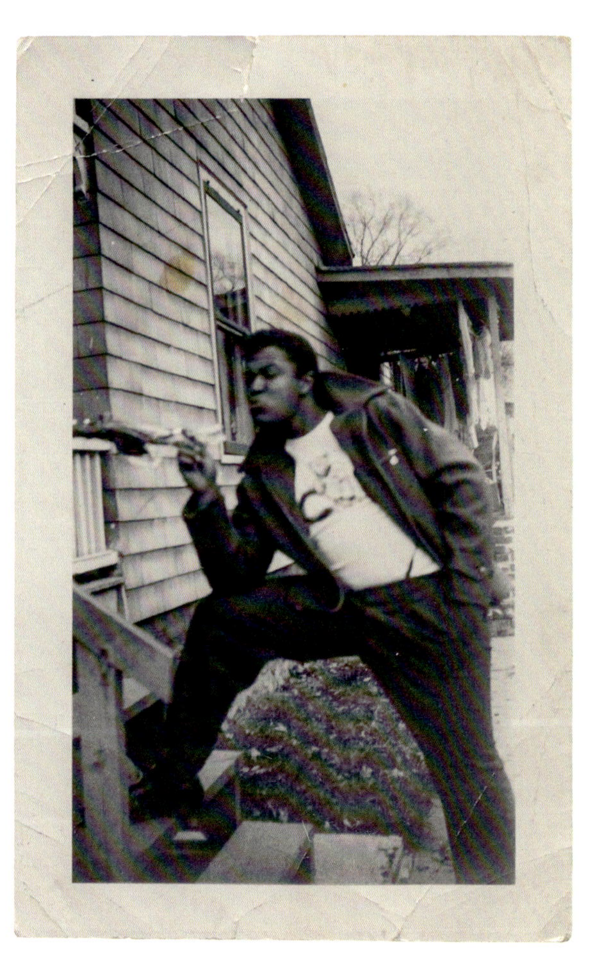

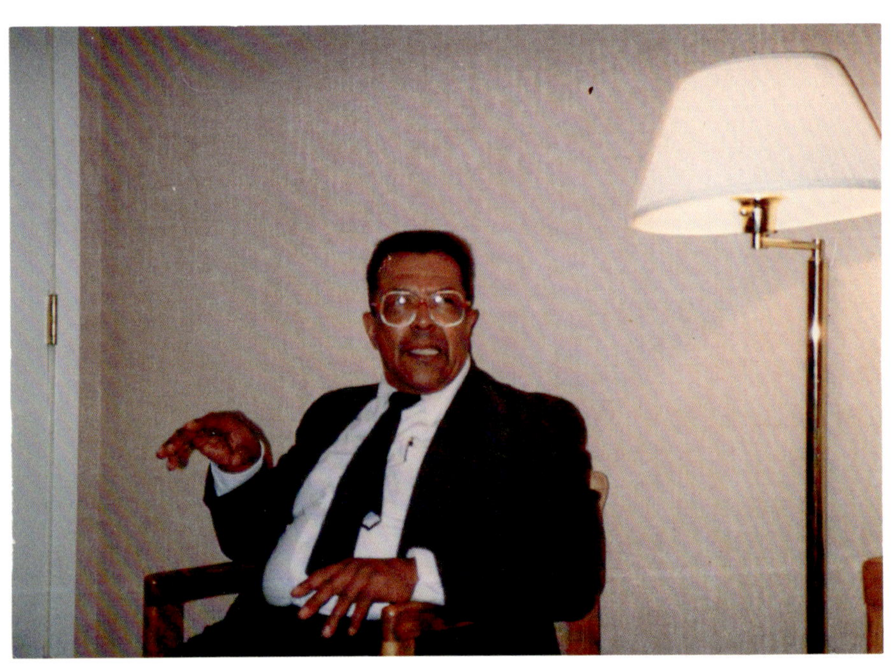

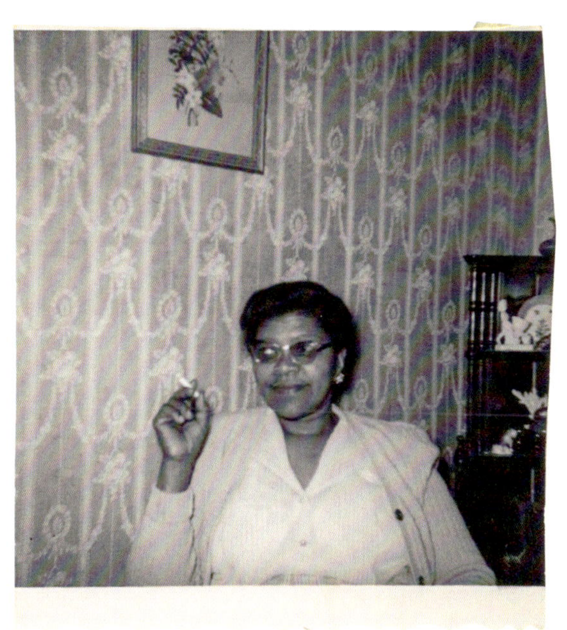

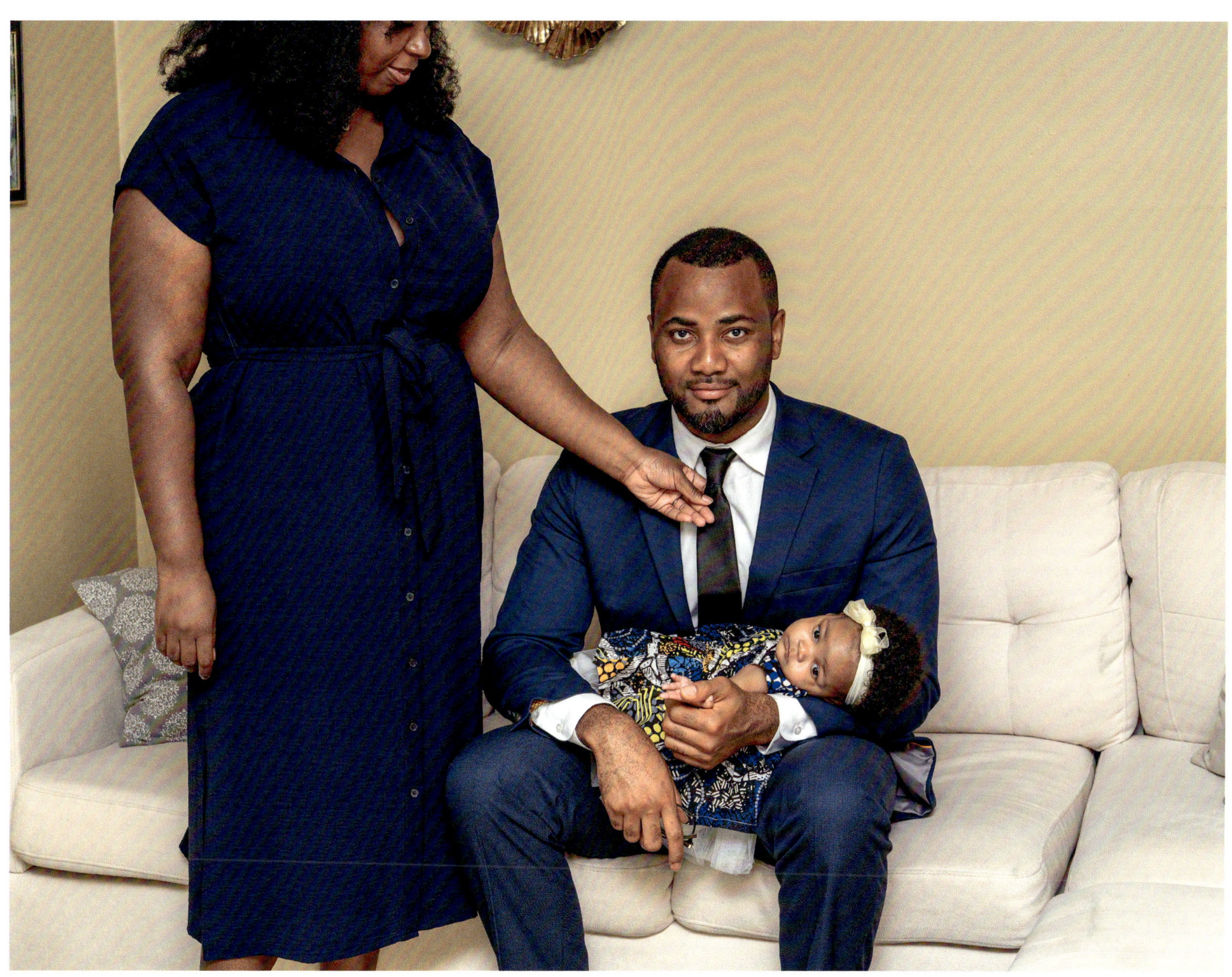

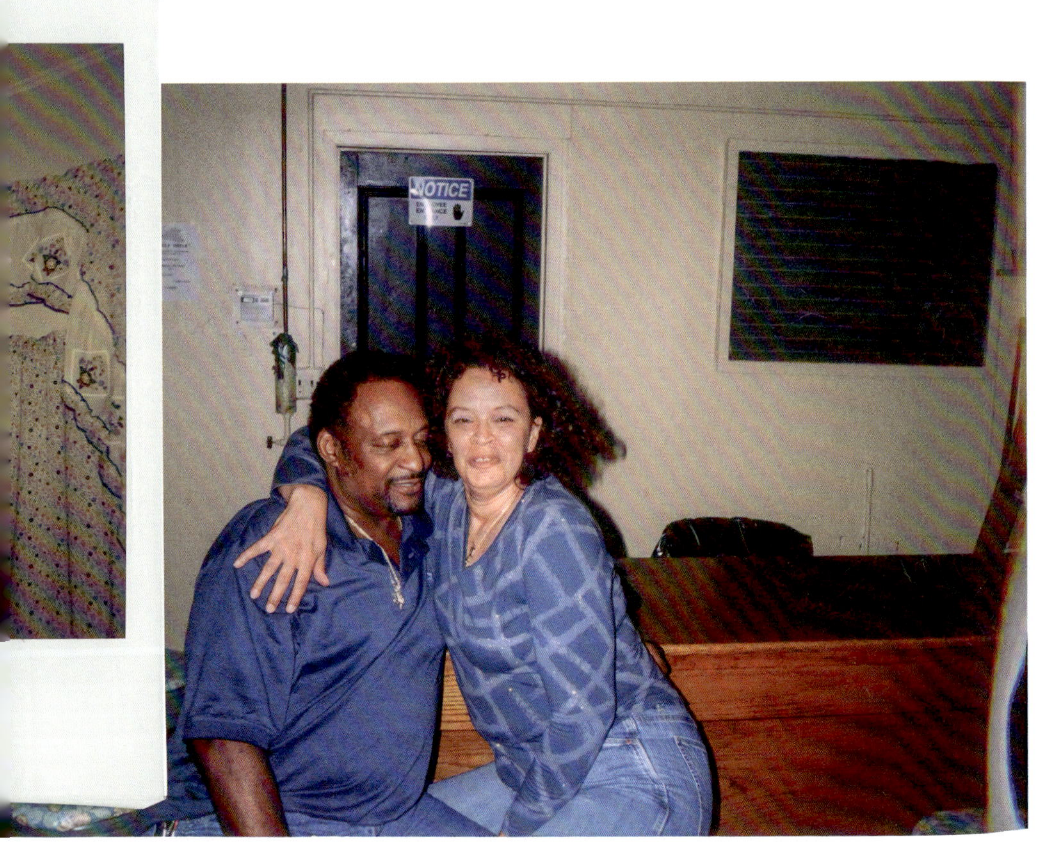

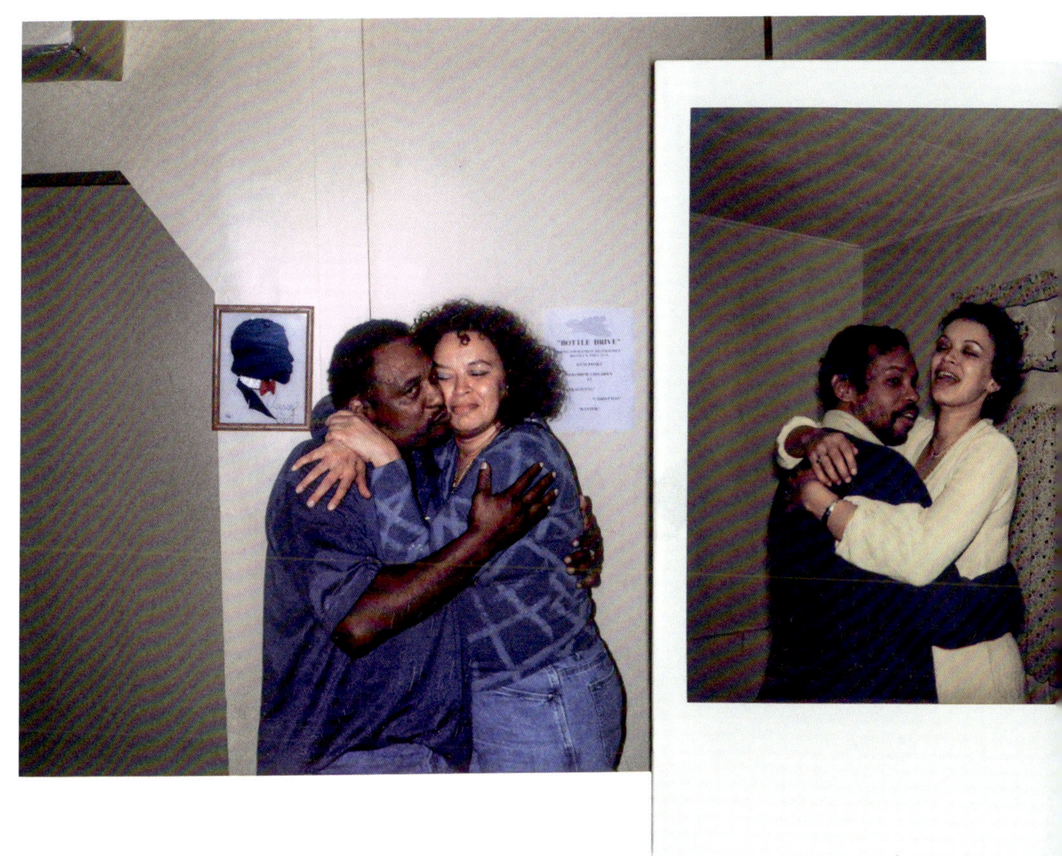

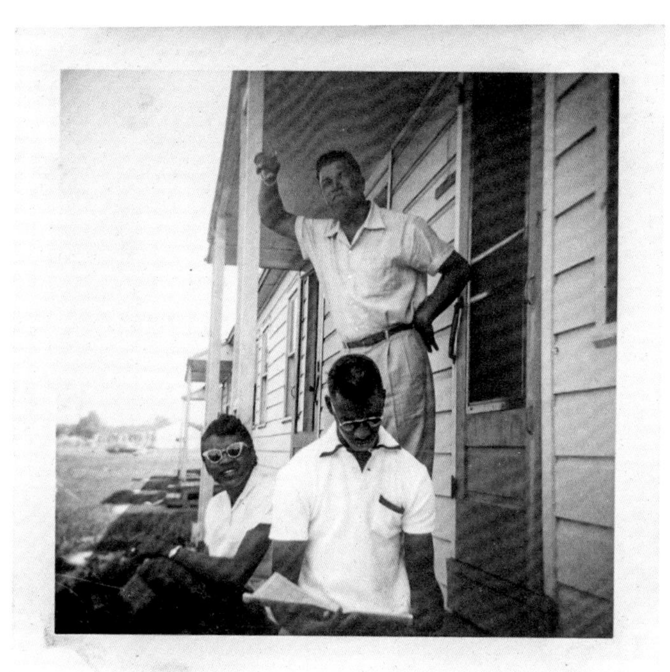

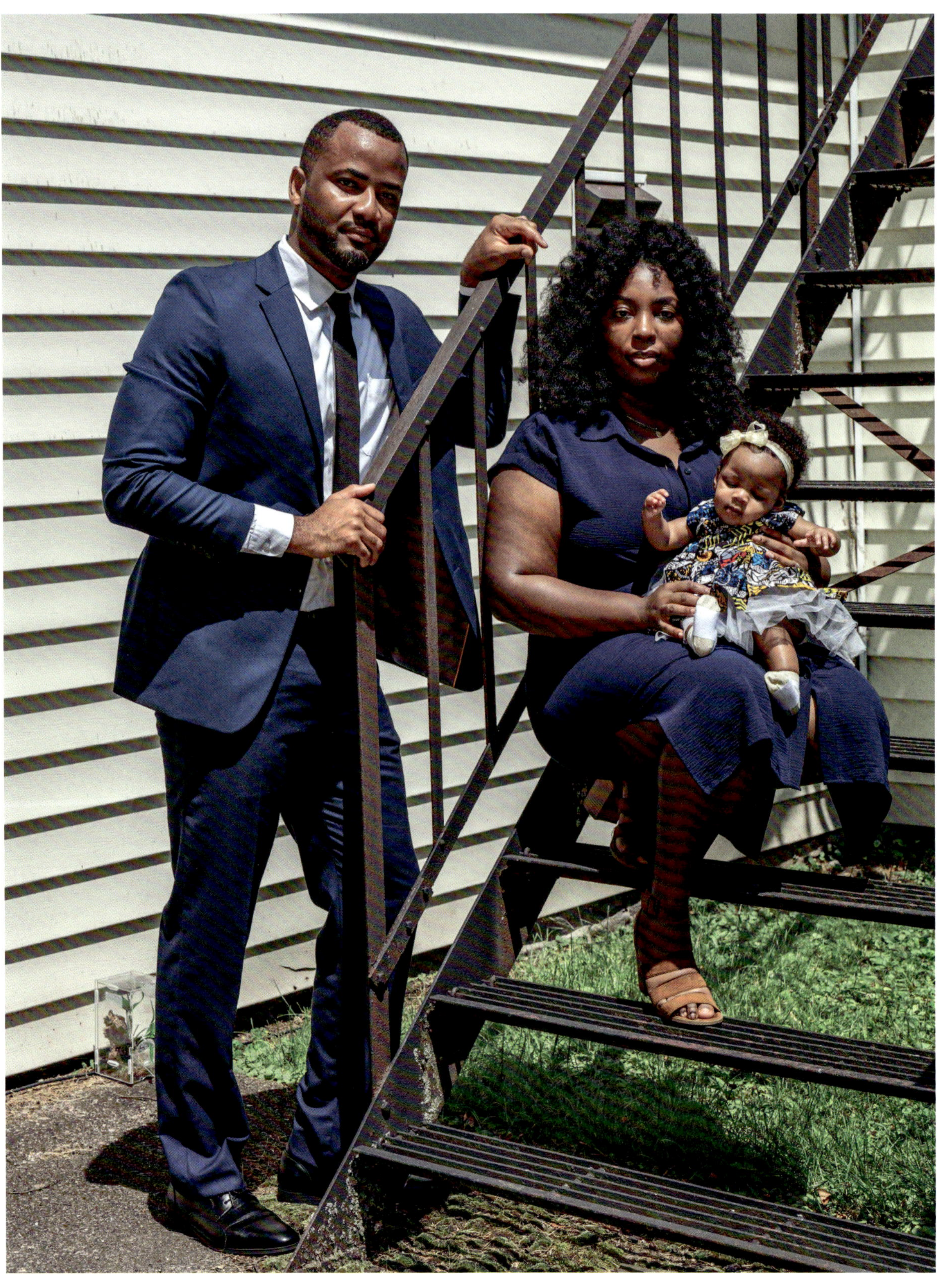

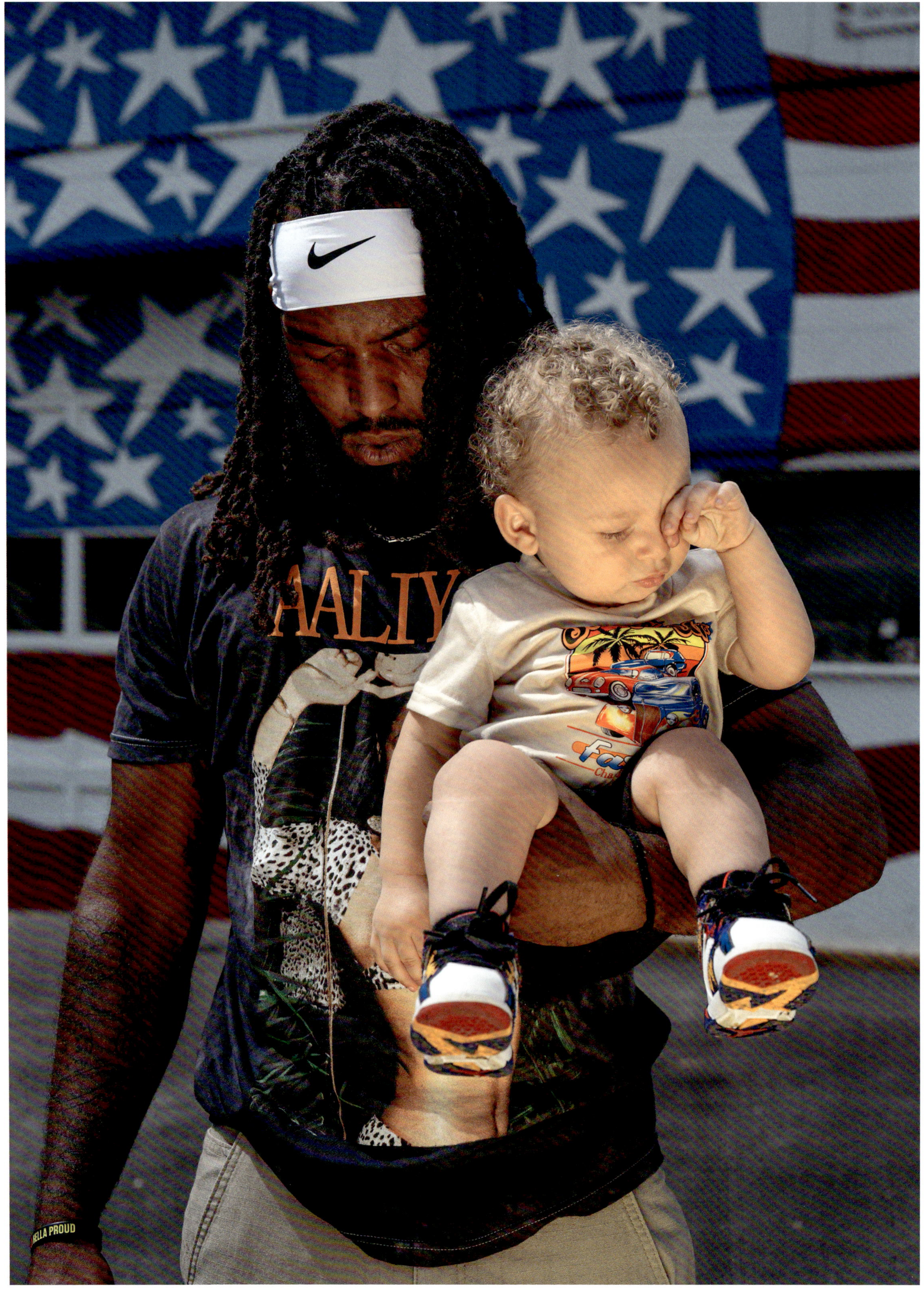
AALIY
BELLA PROUD

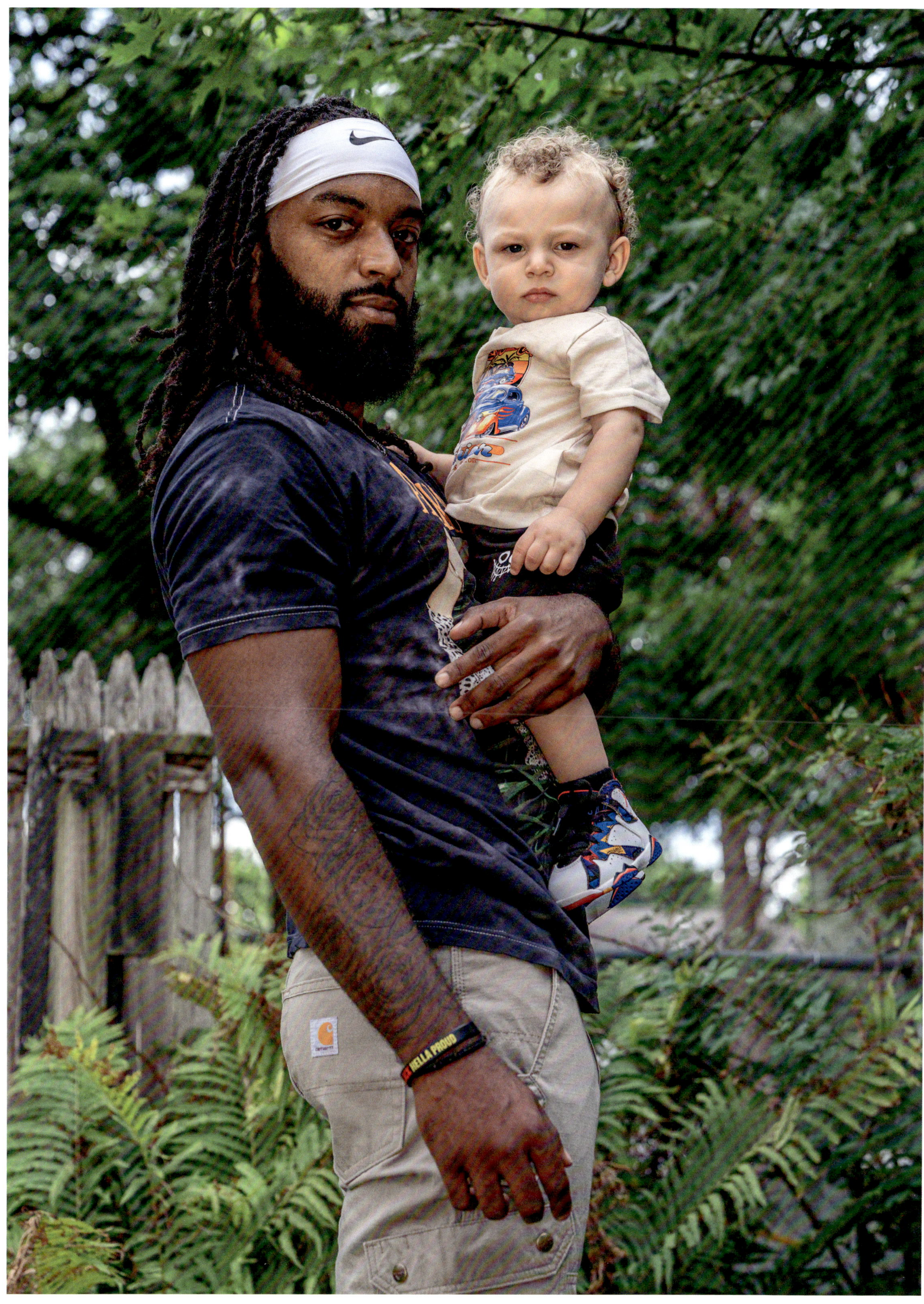

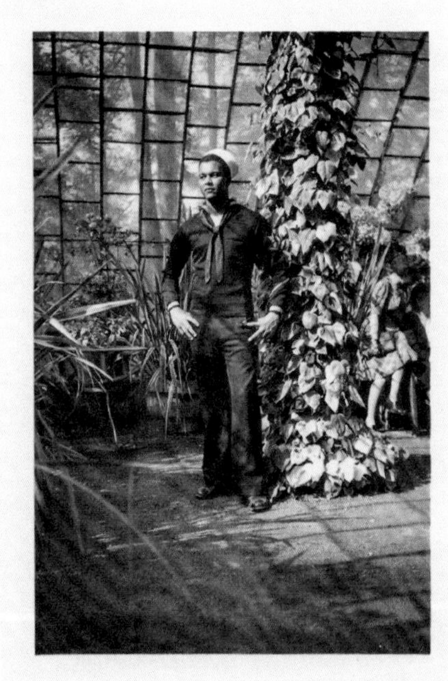

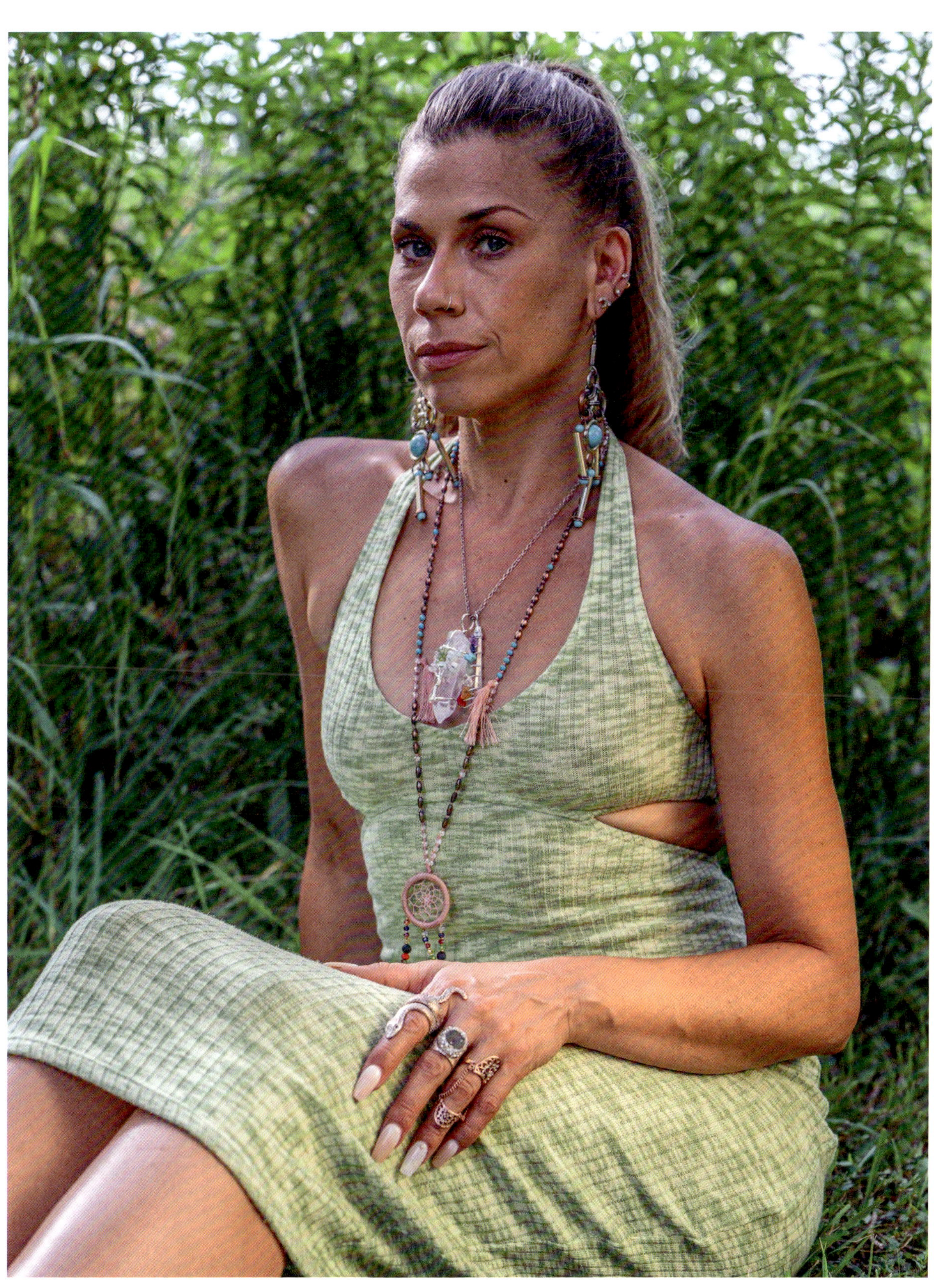

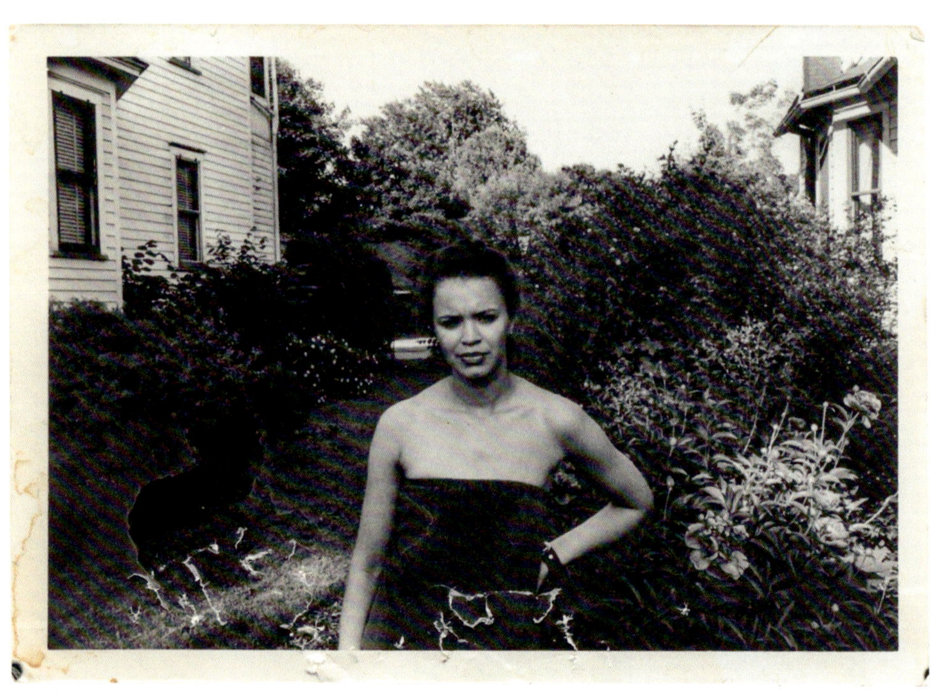

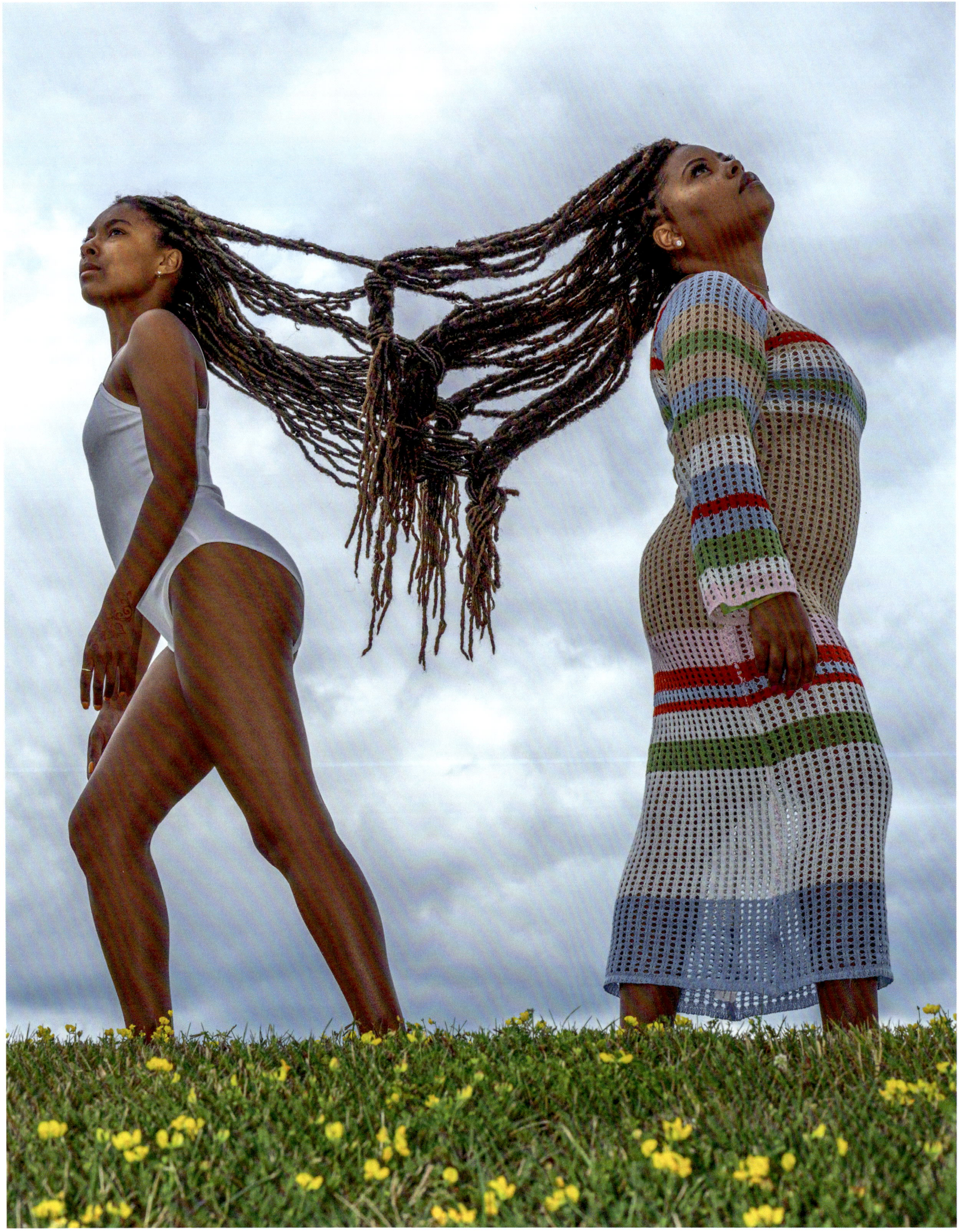

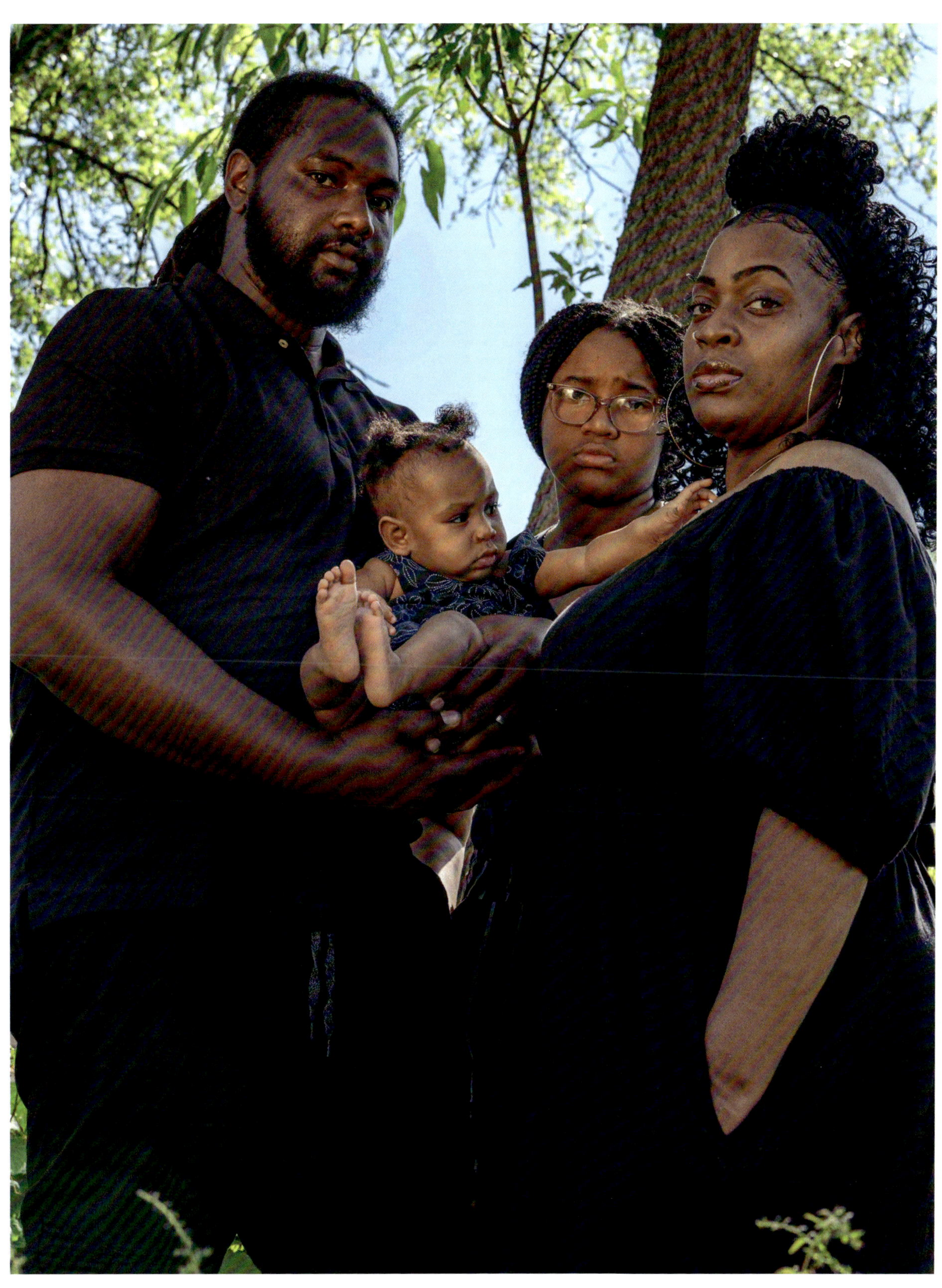

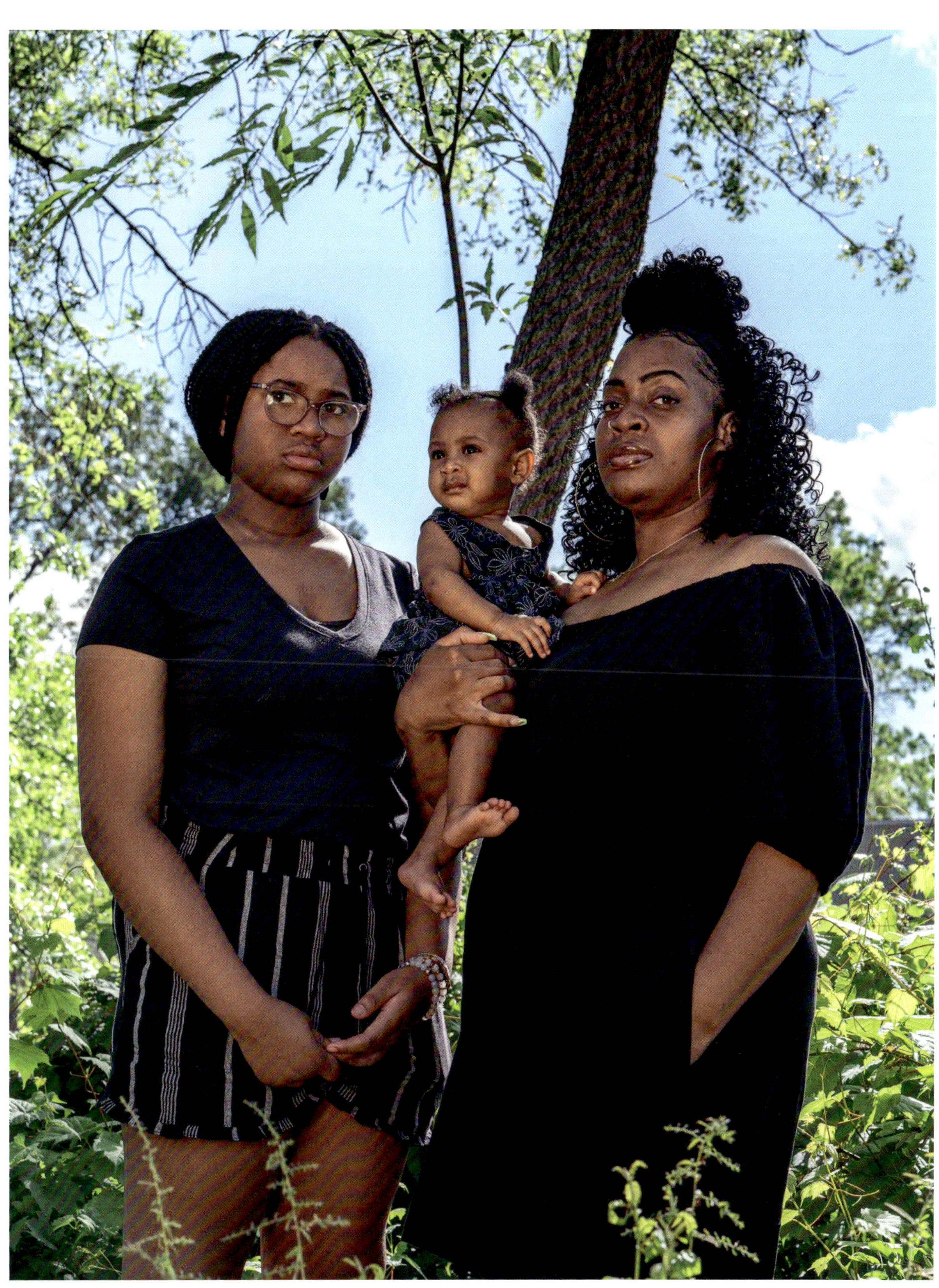

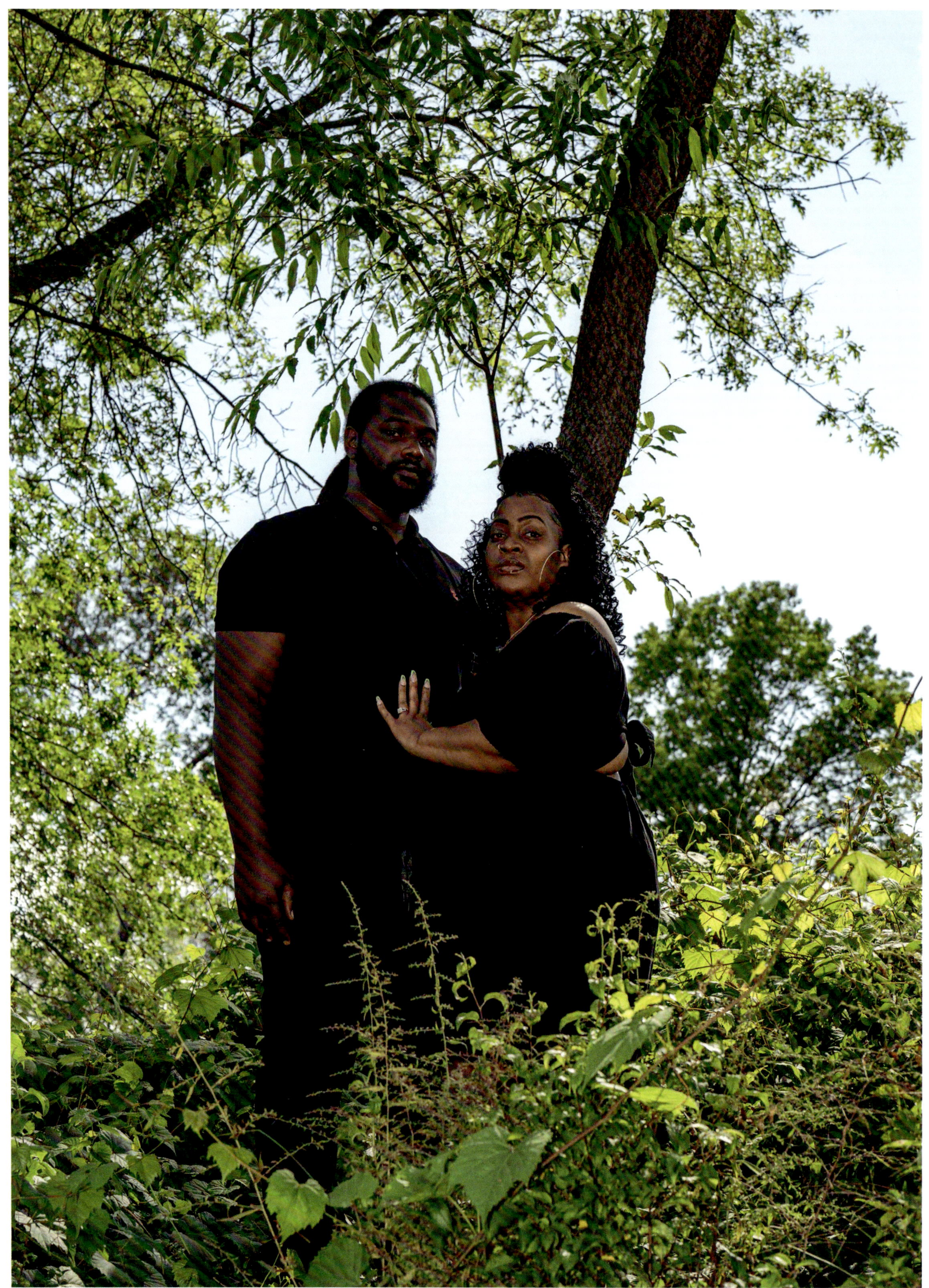

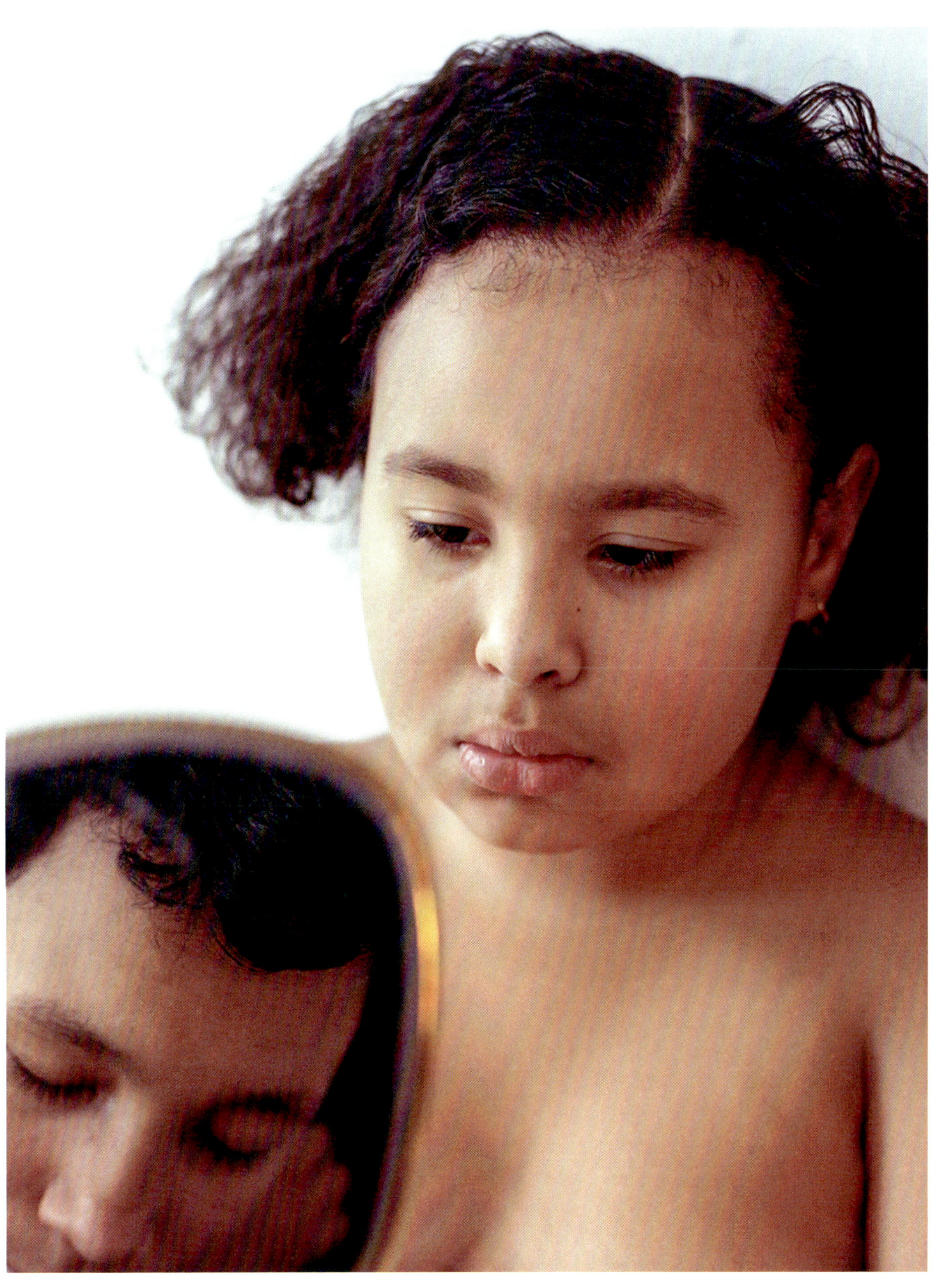

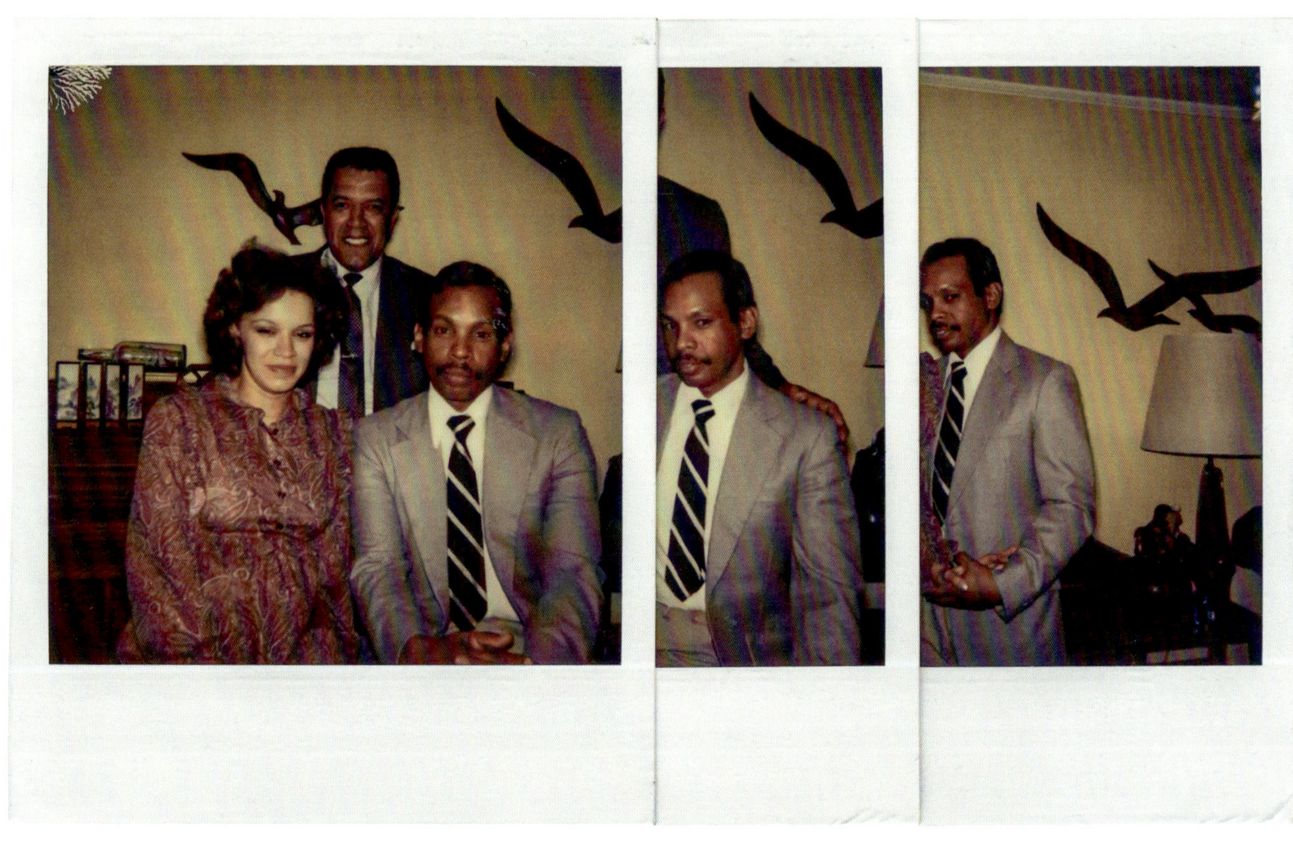

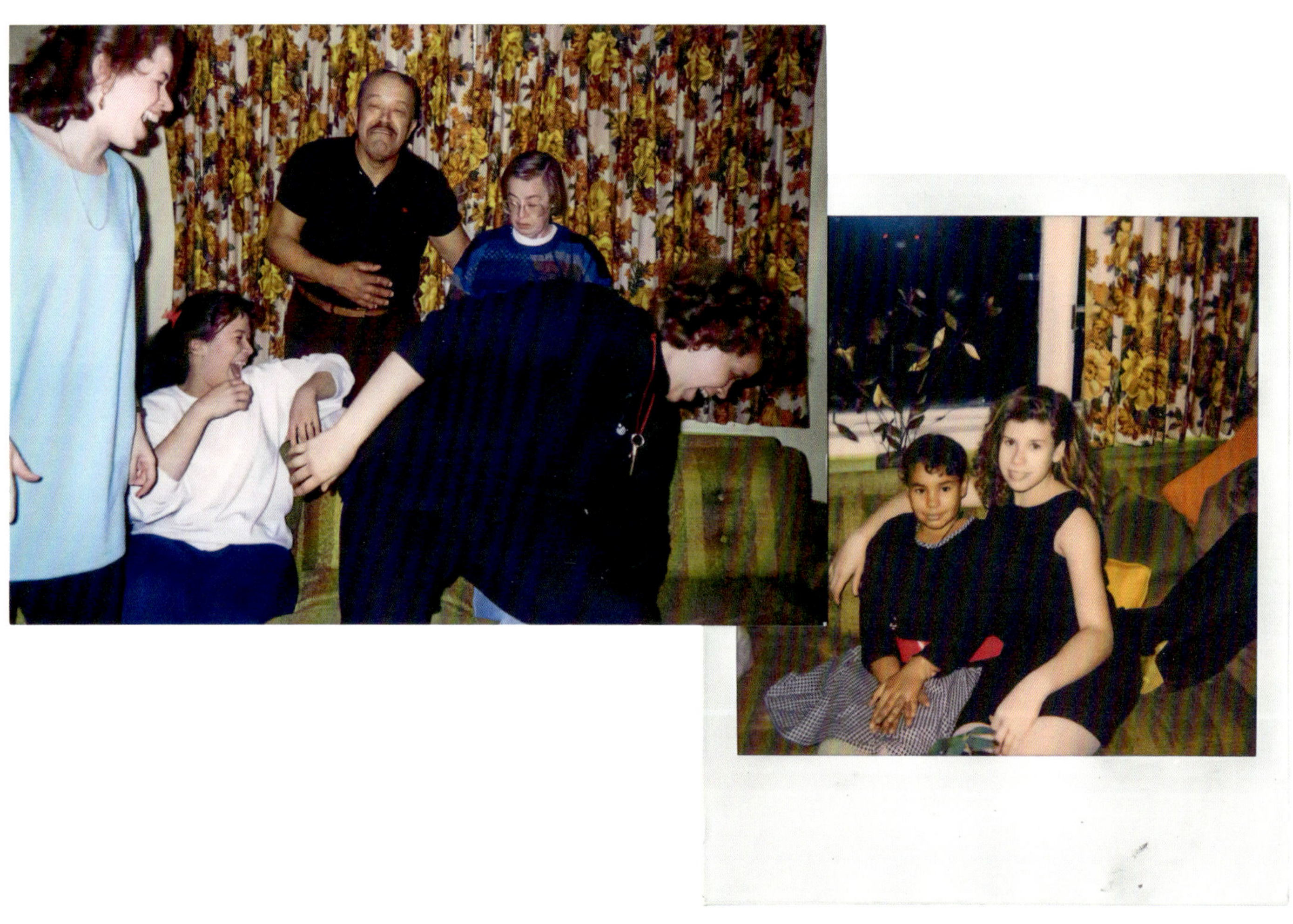

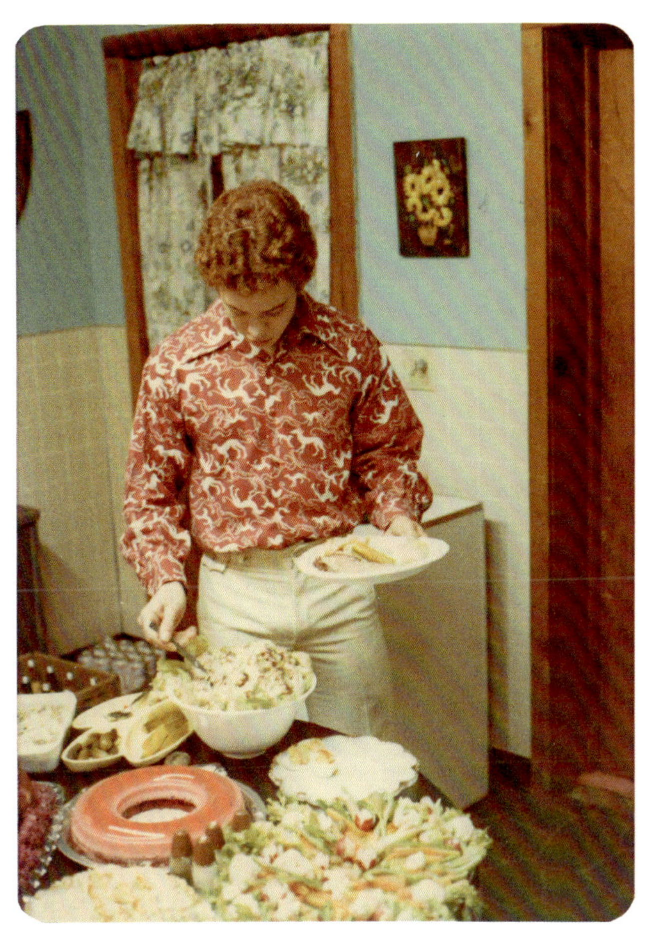

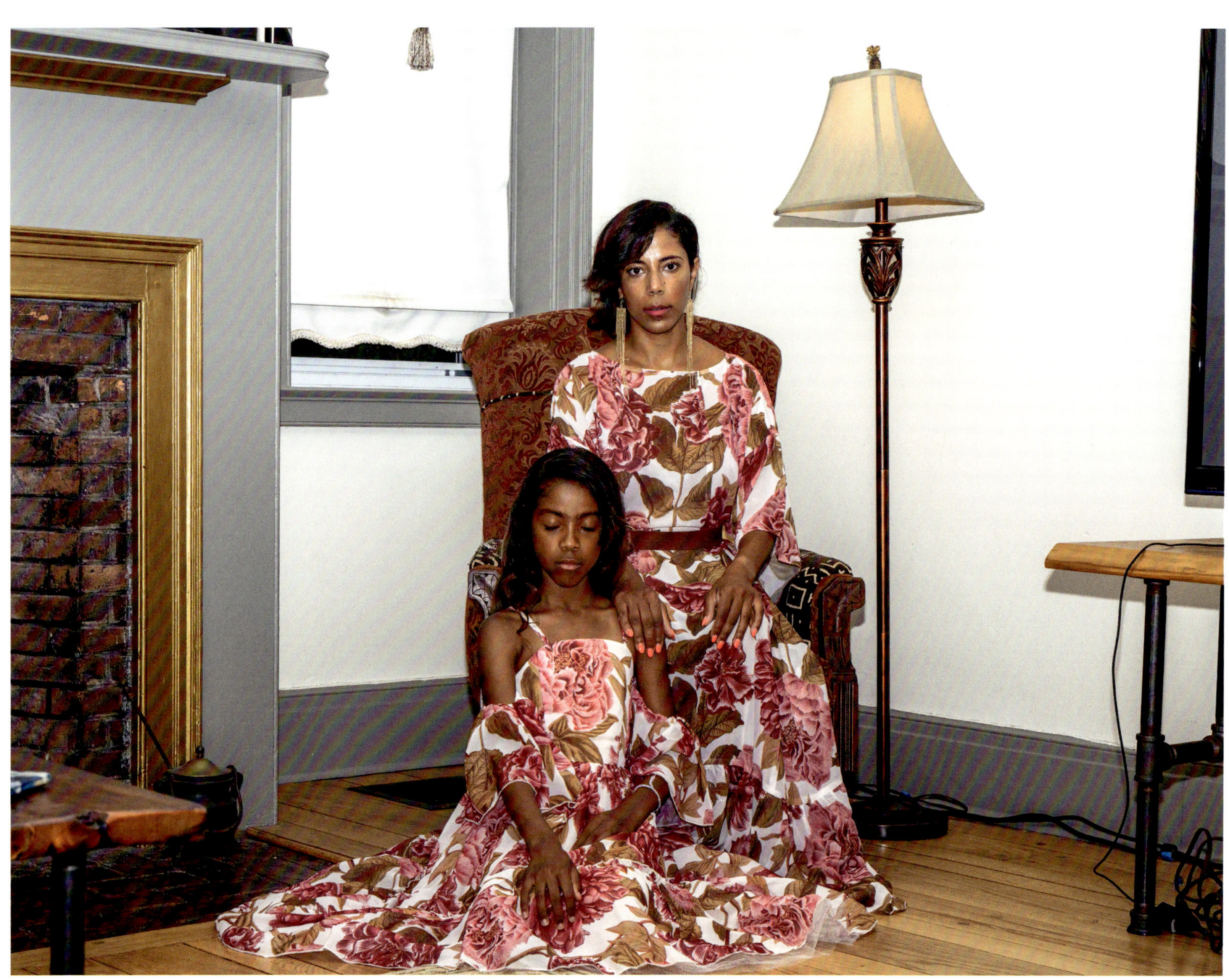

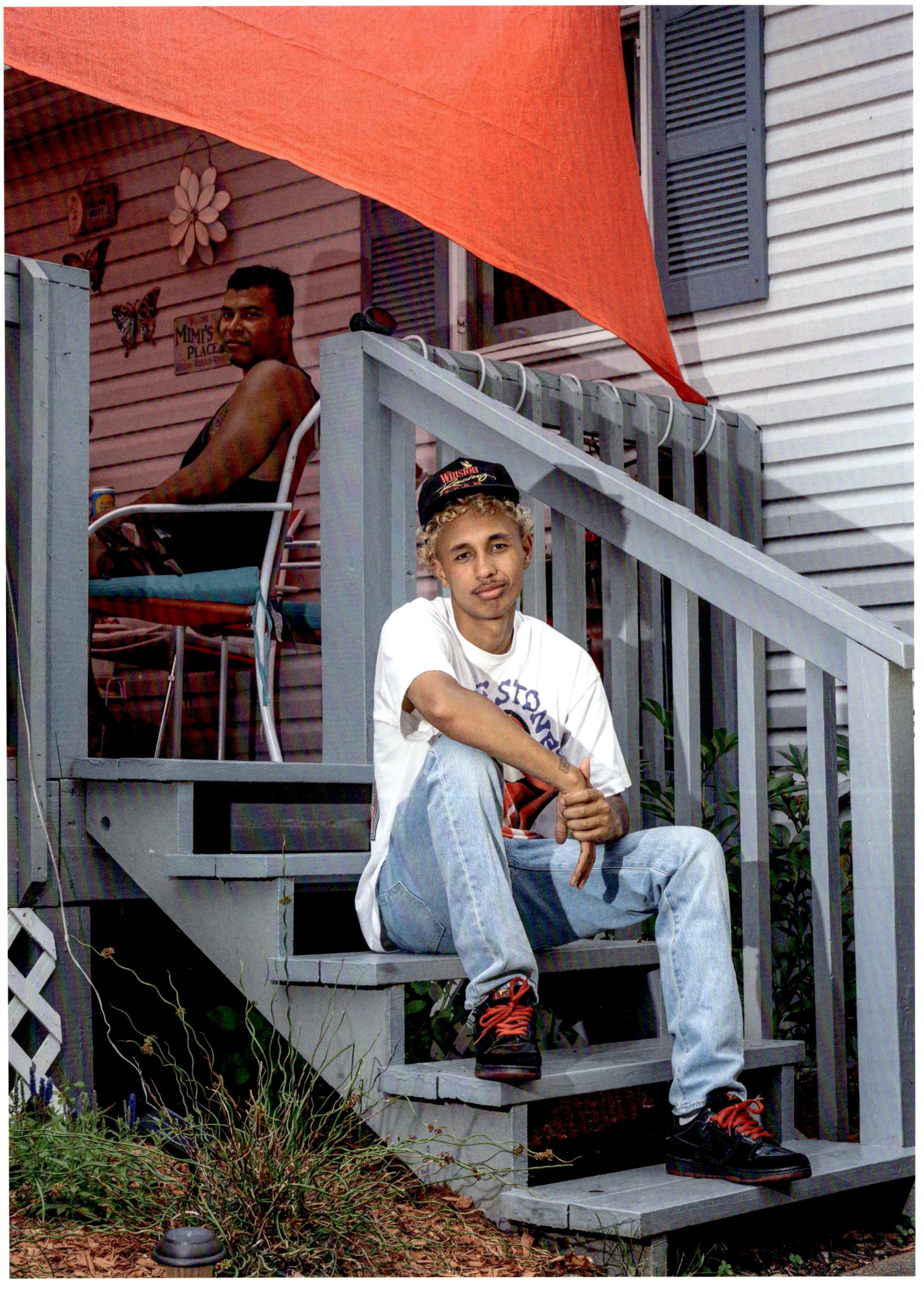

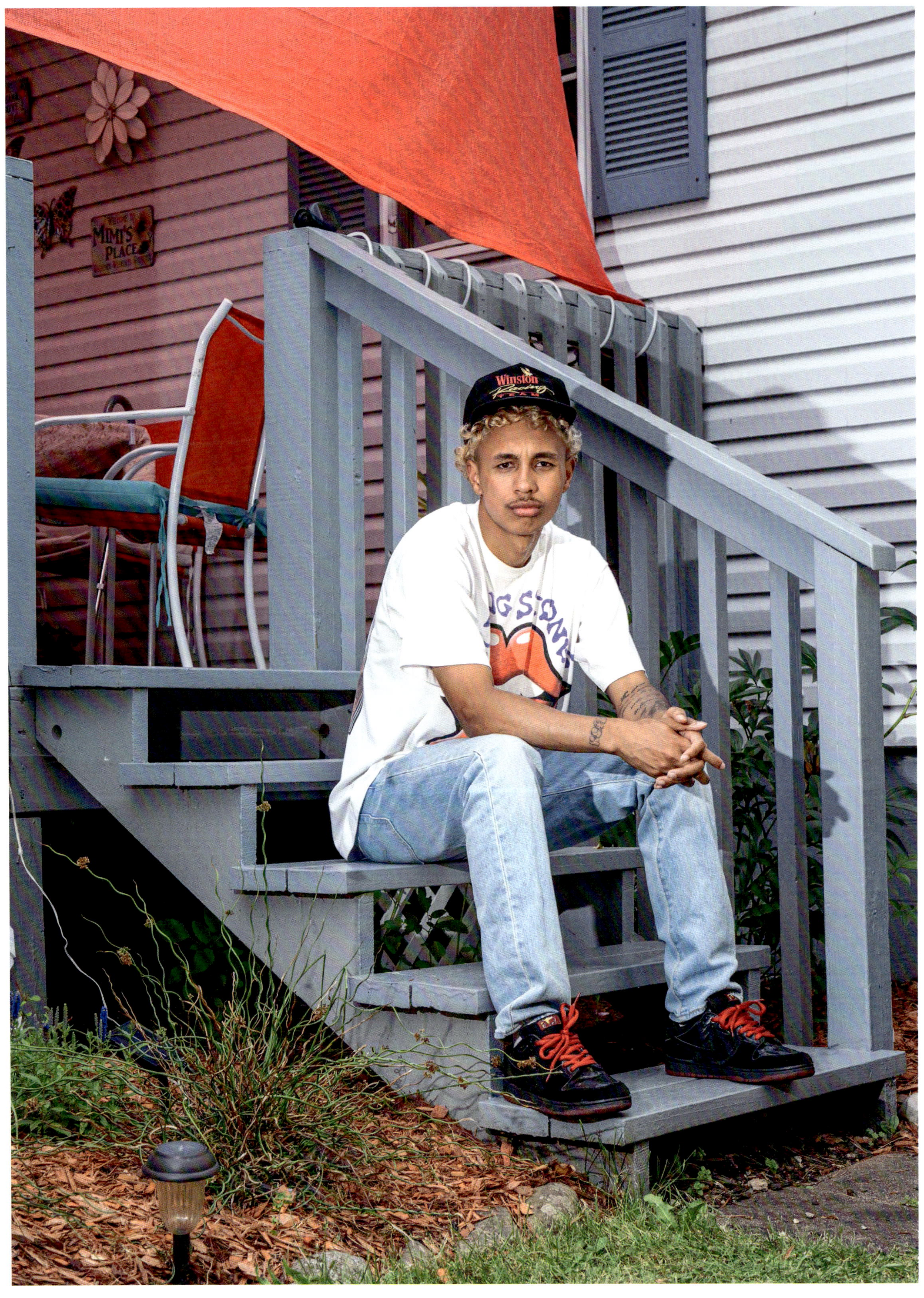

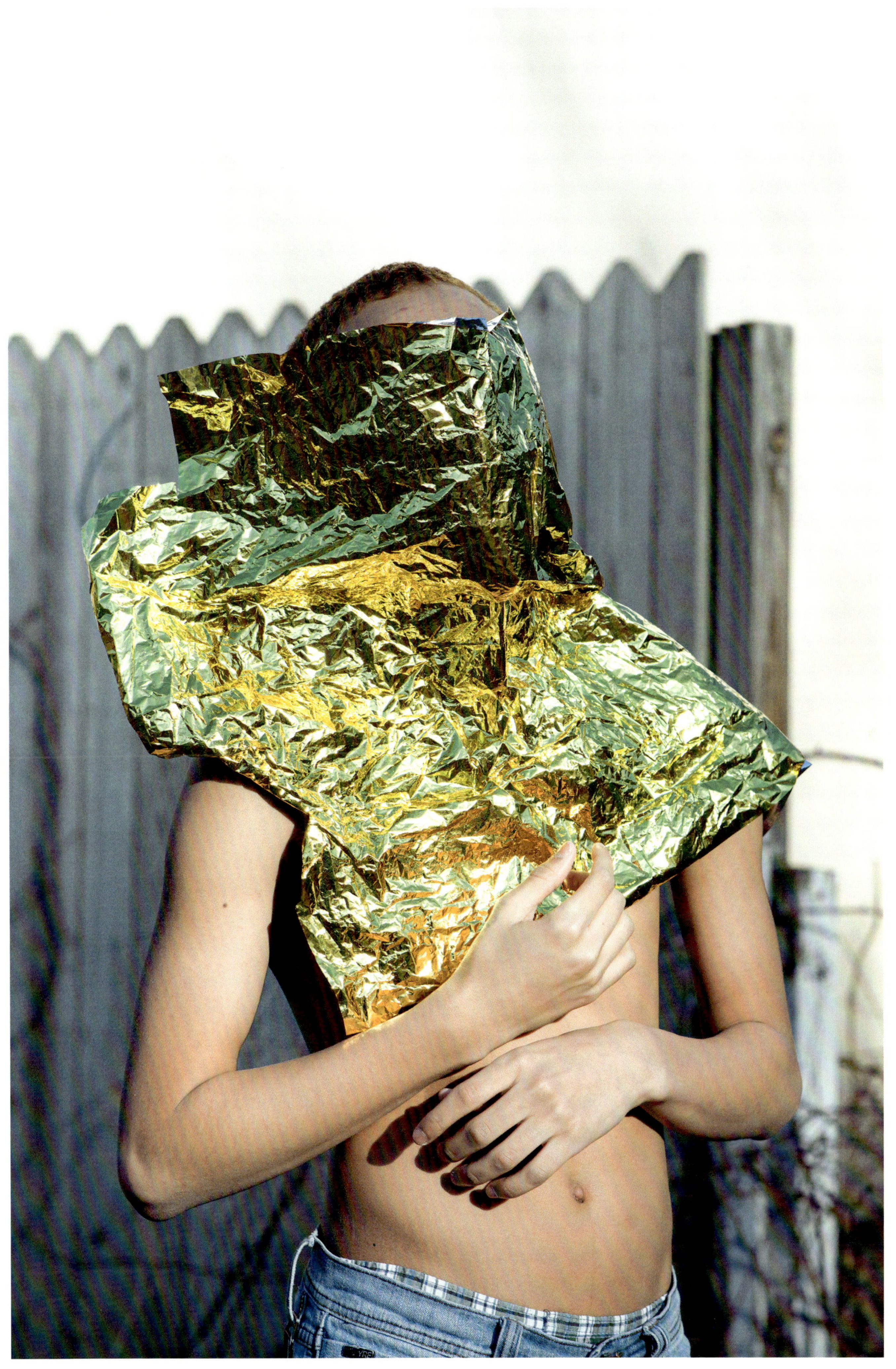

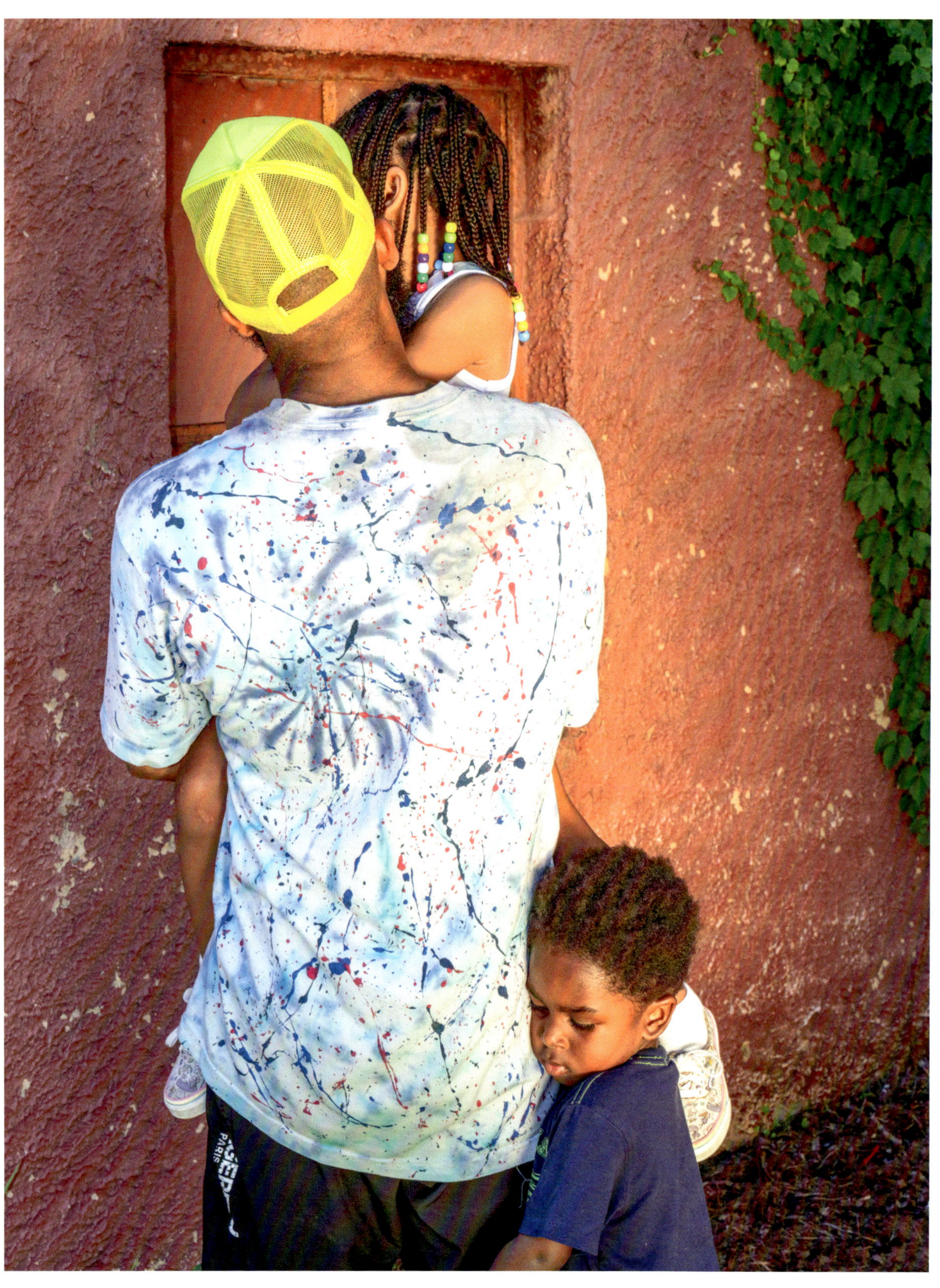

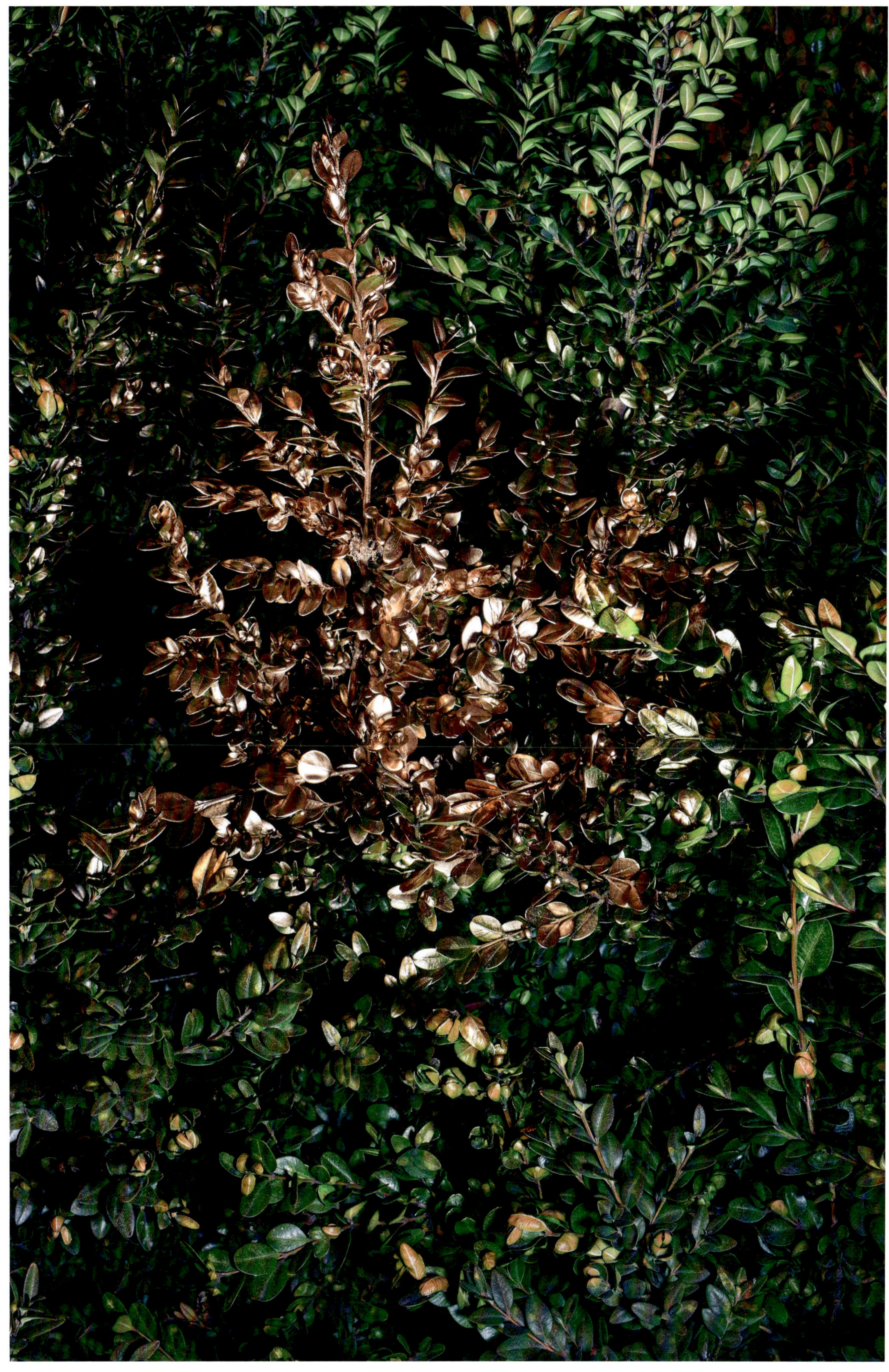

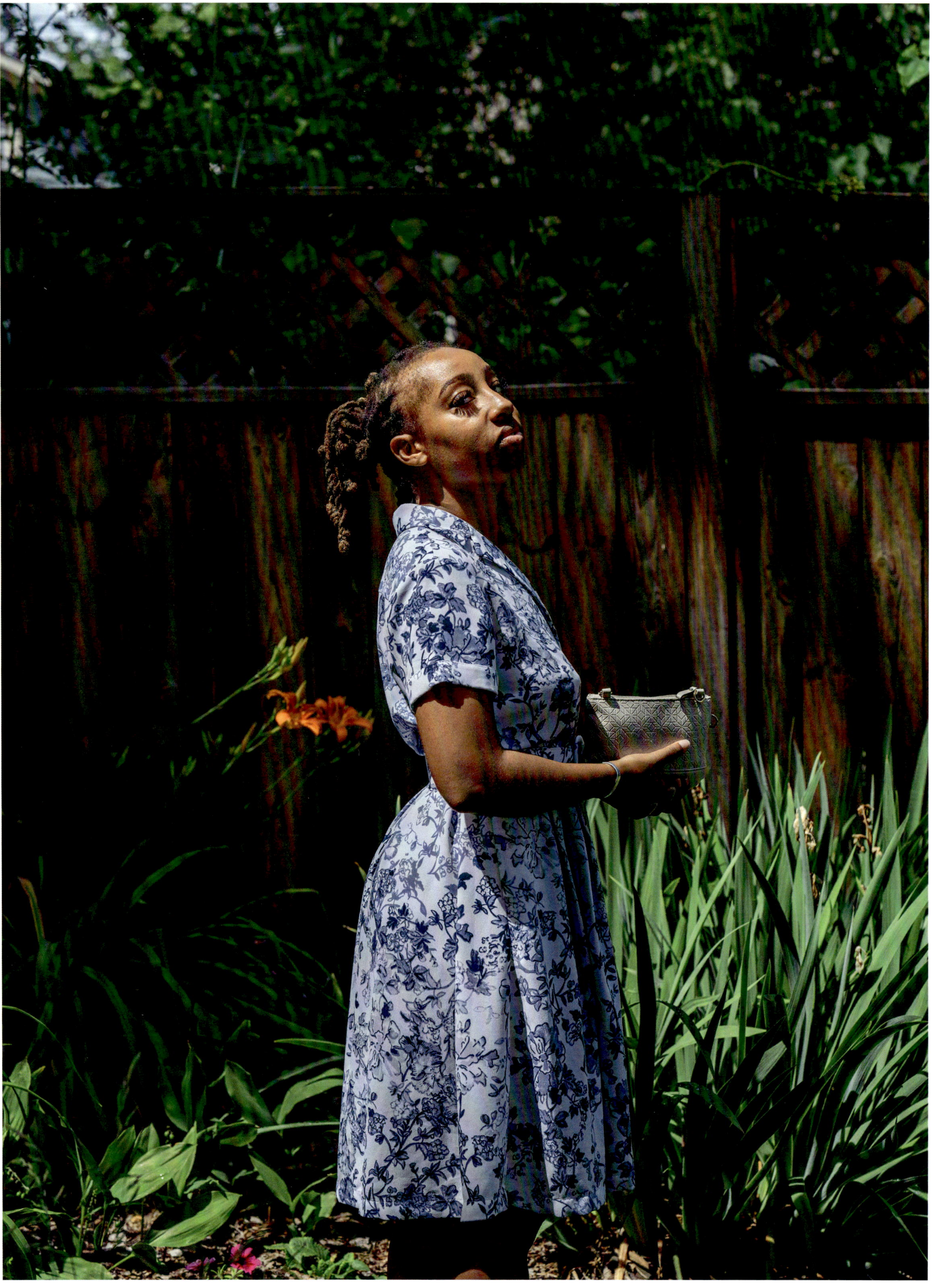

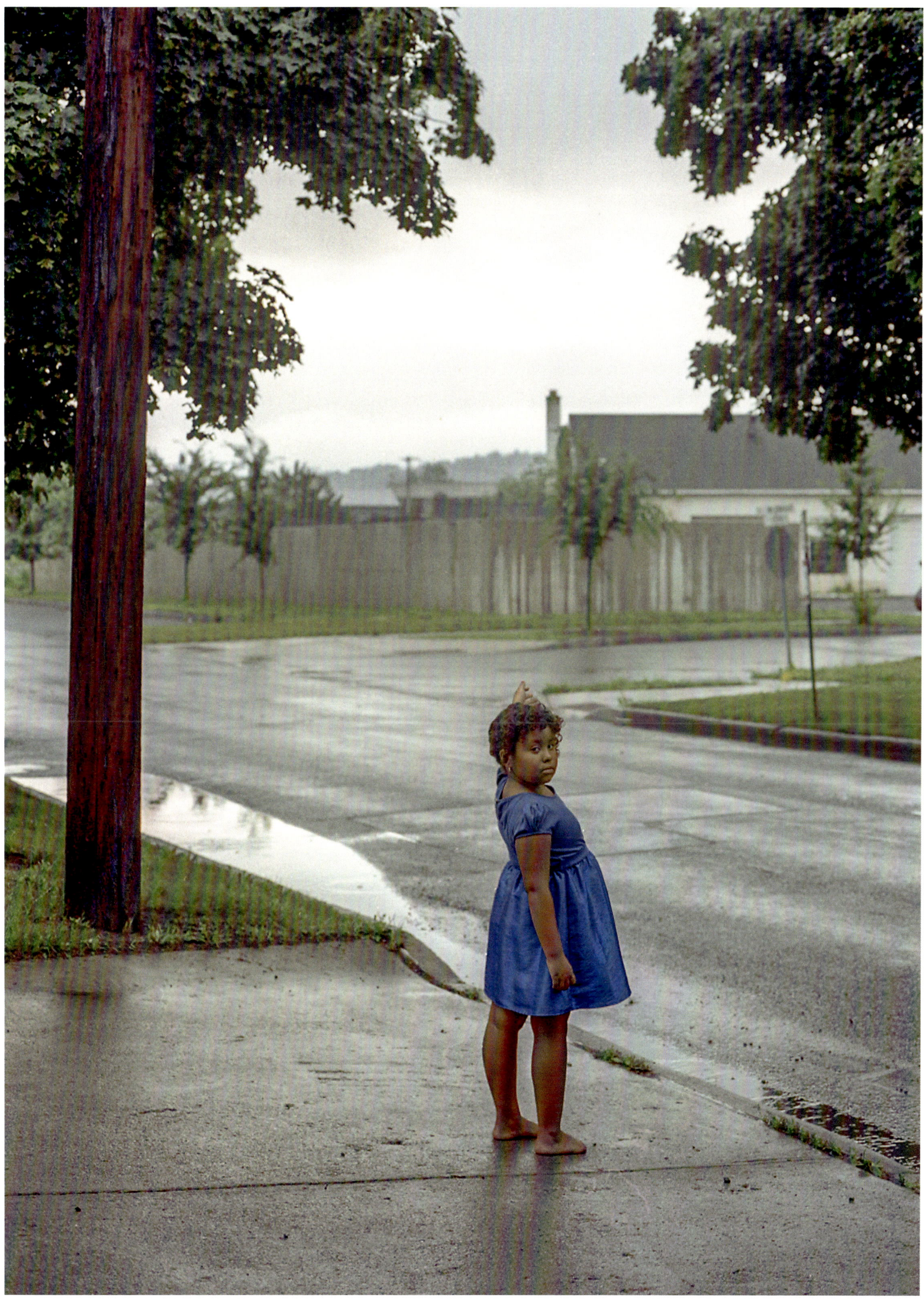

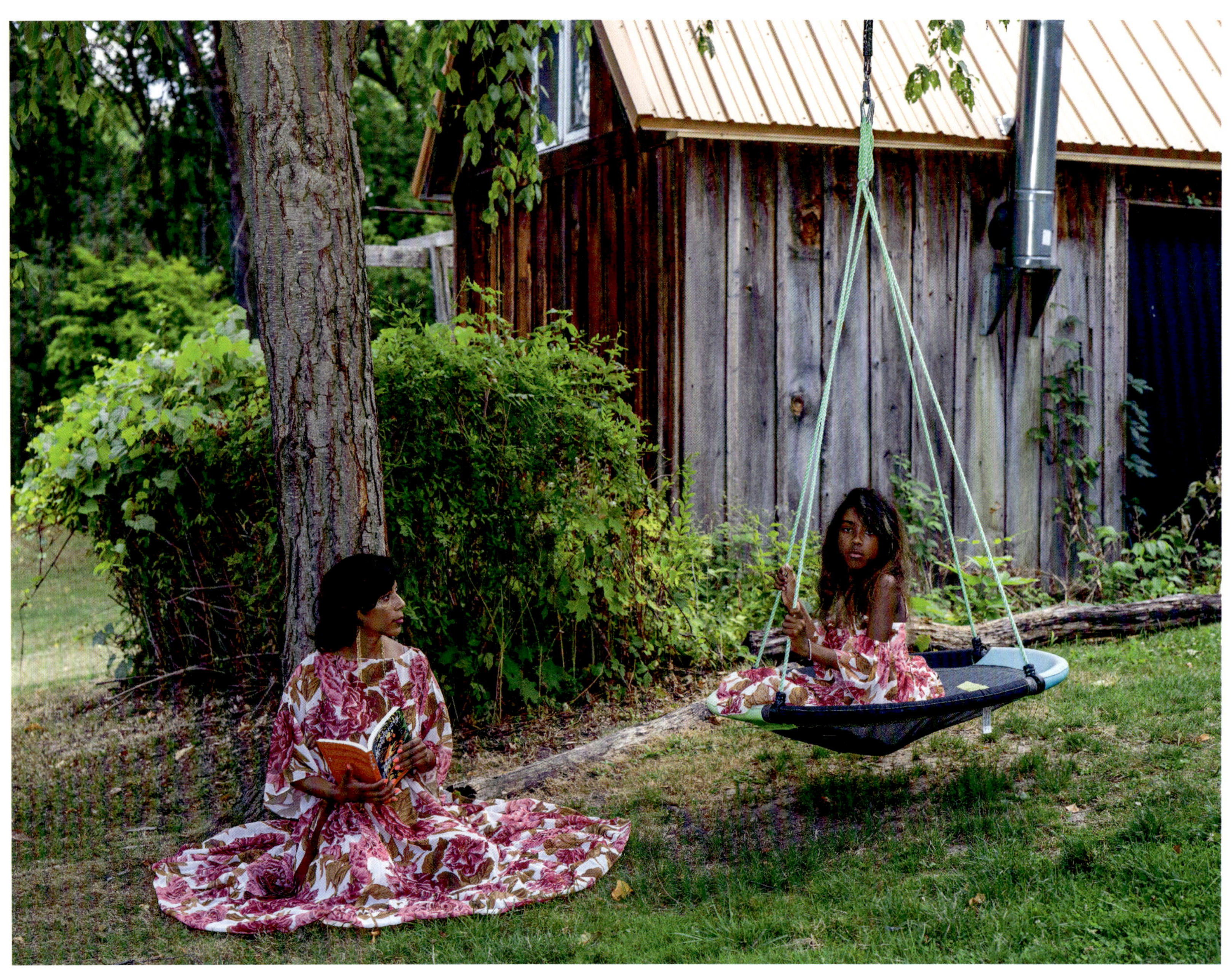

Acknowledgement

My family home at 205 2nd Street was filled with photographs. It is a place
I now remember through photographs, between dreams, and in the crevices
of my heart. I knocked on the door last summer. The screened-in porch of
my childhood seemed so small in my now big body. Or maybe it's because the
house was no longer alive with our collective contagious spirit.

I wonder if the current (white) owners see our memories. It should be
a historical landmark. Birthplace of Beverly J. Martin and Vernon Martin,
the only people who made me feel safe. Summer cookouts in the backyard,
overfilled easter baskets and plastic eggs filled with bills, abundant Christmas
trees, good manners, laughter, and joy. Turkey, ham, or roast depending
on the holiday, Pizza Hut for the impromptu birthday gathering, and always
something sweet. Pop without high fructose corn syrup, fat slugs in the
backyard, that we would melt with salt, like bad witches.

I am a good witch. Recorder of light. My archive produces my memories, time
I forgot without them. But those pictures spoke words. Whispers from behind
the locked china cabinet, observant onlookers spilling out, atop the furniture
they once touched. Did they approve of us? Had we made them proud? Black,
beautiful, successful, still here. Resilient. Proud, and modest. Strong, and soft.
Focused, and free.

LOVE, YOU CAME FROM GREATNESS

IMAGE TEXT ITHACA PRESS

NYDIA BLAS

"In Our Glory: Photography and Black Life" by bell hooks
Conversation between Nydia Blas, Kate Addleman-Frankel, and Cheryl Finley